FROM
SCRATCH

An Introduction to French breads, cheeses, preserves, pickles, charcuterie, condiments, yogurts, sweets, and more

FROM
SCRATCH

An Introduction to French breads, cheeses, preserves, pickles, charcuterie, condiments, yogurts, sweets, and more

LAURENCE AND GILLES LAURENDON, CATHERINE QUÉVREMONT, AND CATHY YTAK

PHOTOGRAPHS BY CHARLOTTE LASCÉVE

LARK

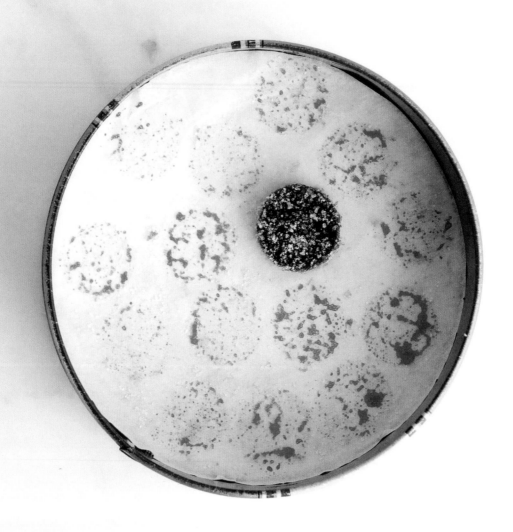

Introduction

Whether it's baking a cake or making a soup, most home cooks are excited by the thought of trying a new recipe. Yet the idea of making bread or yogurt for the first time can be intimidating! Never mind making your own preserves, fresh cheeses, or smoked salmon. When we shop in supermarkets, many of these foods seem like they can only be made by "professionals." Some items, like butter, appear to require special equipment. Other artisan items, such as fresh loaves of bread, seem like they would take years to master.

It's true that some of these recipes will take time and attention to detail before they turn out perfectly. Yet there's a lot to be gained: the satisfaction of producing something new with your own hands and the pleasure of savoring it with friends and family. On the following pages, you'll discover classic French recipes for many items that could become everyday staples in your pantry…which one will you make from scratch?

Contents

CHAPTER 1

Breads & brioches

baguettes, wholegrain bread, biscotti...

MAKING BREAD

fig. 1

fig. 2

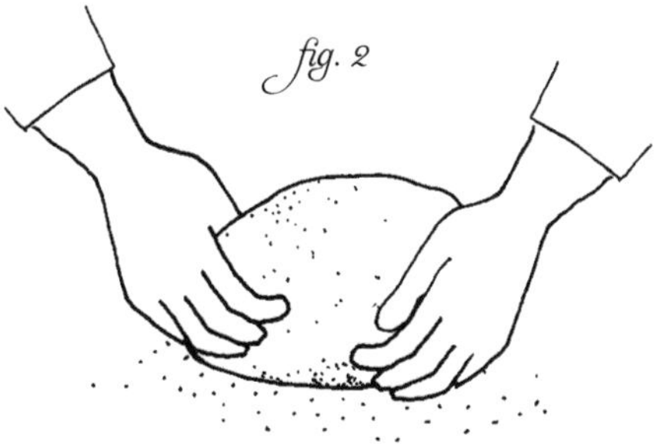

fig. 3

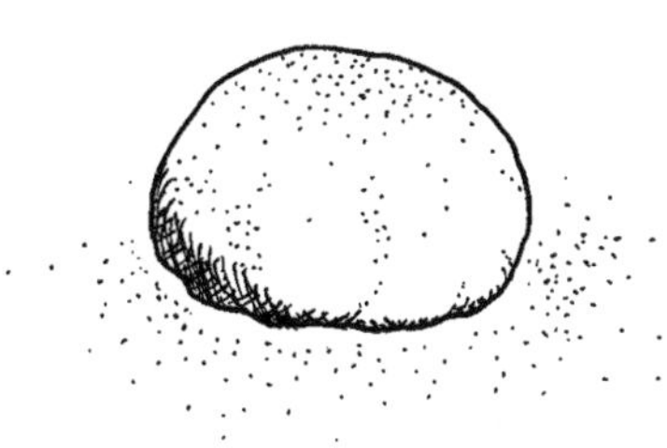

fig. 1 : flour + water + yeast + salt
fig. 2 : mixing and kneading the dough - fig. 3 : setting the dough aside before baking

Handmade White Bread

(Pain blanc à la main)

RECIPE MAKES 1 28-OUNCE (800 G) LOAF
PREP TIME: 30 TO 40 MINUTES
SET ASIDE: 1 HOUR 25 MINUTES TO 2 HOURS 25 MINUTES
BAKING TIME: 40 TO 50 MINUTES

4 cups (500 g) high-gluten white wheat flour,
preferably organic

1¼ cups (280-300 ml) non-chlorinated water

1¼ tablespoons dehydrated yeast (also known as fermentable wheat yeast, sold at natural food stores) or ½ tablespoon of instant baker's yeast (sold at supermarkets)

½ tablespoon (8 g) salt

1. Put the flour, salt, yeast, and lemon juice into a
large mixing bowl, and add the water. Mix all of the
ingredients together with your hands and then set
the mixture aside so that the flour can rehydrate.
Wait 10 minutes.

2. Next, scrape the flour from the edges of the bowl
toward the center and work it into the dough with
your hands. Mix vigorously. Then, with the palms of
both hands, knead the dough in a regular movement.
It should become very sticky. If it doesn't, add 1
teaspoon of water. Knead for 15 to 25 minutes. The
dough should become increasingly elastic and less
sticky. If necessary, add water and a little flour.

3. You should now have a well-formed ball of dough.
Leave it in the mixing bowl and cover it with a
dishtowel. In order to rise, it must remain at a
temperature of at least 72°F. Put it in a safe spot
where it won't get bumped and let it sit for 30 to
45 minutes (a little more in winter, a little less in
summer).

4. Knead the dough again for a few minutes, making
sure you eliminate any bubbles that form.

5. Next, shape the bread. On a smooth work surface
dusted with flour, spread the dough out so that it
forms a rectangle. Fold the dough in two by pulling
it back toward you, and press the edges together.
Fold the dough and press the edges together a
second time. Then roll the ball of dough into a
cylinder. Cover it with a dishtowel that's been
sprinkled with flour and water and set it aside with
the seam on top for 45 to 90 minutes, depending
on the temperature of the room.

6. Pre-heat the oven to 425°F for 10 minutes.

7. Carefully tip the dough onto a baking plate,
making sure the seam is on top. Be very careful when
working with the dough—it's fragile. Score the top
of the dough lengthwise with a knife at a 30° angle.

8. Put the dough in the oven. Then pour a bit of
boiling water into a dripping pan, put the pan in
the oven, and immediately close the oven door
to keep the steam inside. Steam is the secret to
baking bread with a golden crust. Bake the dough
for 40 to 50 minutes.

9. Remove the bread from the oven and let it cool
on a rack.

When is the dough ready?

To determine whether or not the ball of dough is ready
to go into the oven, poke a hole in it with your finger. If
the hole disappears immediately, you should wait a bit.
If it disappears slowly, the dough is ready. If it doesn't
disappear, the dough has risen too much.

Whole-Grain Bread

(Pain complet)

RECIPE MAKES 1 2-POUND (750 G) LOAF
BREAD MACHINE SETTING: DOUGH
PREP TIME (NOT COUNTING KNEADING AND MACHINE RISING):
   15 MINUTES
SET ASIDE: 20 TO 40 MINUTES
BAKING TIME: 40 MINUTESABOUT

1¼ cups (270 to 300 ml) water: adjust according to
   machine (see Hydration Rate box below)

2½ cups (300 g) unbleached light whole-wheat flour

1¼ cups (150 g) dark whole-wheat flour

2½ teaspoons (8 g) dehydrated yeast (also referred to as
   fermentable wheat yeast; sold at natural-food stores)
   or 1 teaspoon (4 g) instant baker's yeast (sold at
   supermarkets)

1½ teaspoons (6 g) salt

1 teaspoon sugar

1 tablespoon olive oil or butter

1 teaspoon lemon juice

1. Put all of the ingredients into the mixing pan of
the machine. Make sure the salt doesn't touch the
baker's yeast (if it does, it may deactivate the yeast).

2. Put the mixing pan into the machine, close the lid,
and select the dough setting.

3. After 10 minutes, check the consistency of the
dough and scrape the sides of the mixing pan with
a flexible spatula if necessary. The dough should
already be well formed. If it sticks to the sides of the
pan and is very soft, add 2 rounded teaspoons
(10 g) of flour. If the dough tears and can't be
formed into a nice, smooth ball, add 2 teaspoons
(10 ml) of water.

4. When the dough is ready, take it out of the pan
and place it on a smooth work surface dusted with
flour. Shape the dough into a flat pancake, and then
fold it under so that it forms a nice ball. Put it in
a mixing bowl, making sure its seam is on top, and
cover it with a dishtowel that's slightly moist and
thoroughly dusted with flour. Let the dough rise in
the bowl for 20 to 40 minutes.

5. Preheat your oven to 425°F for 10 minutes.

6. Put the dough on a baking sheet, cut a star or
a cross on top of it, and put it into the oven. Then
pour a bit of boiling water into a dripping pan, put
the pan in the oven, and immediately close the oven
door to keep the steam inside. Steam is the secret to
baking bread with a golden crust.

7. When the bread is thoroughly baked, take it out
of the oven. Let it cool on a rack and enjoy!

Hand Kneading

*The recipes in this book that are made with bread
machines can also be prepared entirely by hand. Just follow
the instructions for making Handmade White Bread on
page 10, adjusting water quantities as needed.*

Hydration rate

The success of your bread depends largely on achieving
the right water-to-flour ratio. Known as the hydration
rate, this ratio will vary depending on the machine you're
using, the type of flour you're baking with (whole-grain
flour requires more water), and the temperature of the
room (the hotter the temperature, the more water that's
needed). Each recipe in this book includes a quantity
scale. Start with the smallest quantity and keep refining
until you get satisfactory results.

Wheat-Stalk Baguettes

(Baguette épis)

RECIPE MAKES 4 BAGUETTES
BREAD MACHINE SETTING: DOUGH OR PIZZA DOUGH
PREP TIME (NOT COUNTING MACHINE KNEADING AND RISING):
   10 MINUTES
SET ASIDE: 30 MINUTES
NOTE: YOU'LL NEED TO PREPARE A POOLISH (SEE BOX BELOW)
   A DAY IN ADVANCE, OR IN THE MORNING FOR USE IN
   THE EVENING.

1 rounded cup (150 g) all-purpose or high-gluten wheat flour

¾ cup (150 ml) water

1 small teaspoon (2 g) dehydrated yeast (also known as
   fermentable wheat yeast; sold at natural-food stores) or
   1 pinch instant baker's yeast (sold at supermarkets)

For the dough:

¾ cup (between 210 and 250 ml) water: adjust according
   to machine (see Hydration Rate box, page 12)

1¾ rounded cups (225 g) all-purpose or high-gluten wheat
   flour

1¾ rounded cups (225 g) spelt flour

2 teaspoons (6 g) dehydrated yeast or 1 teaspoon (3 g)
   instant baker's yeast

2 teaspoons (8 g) salt

1 teaspoon lemon juice

1. Prepare the poolish by mixing the flour and
the water. Cover it with a dishtowel and set it in a
warm place.

2. The following day (or on the evening of the same
day), put the poolish into the mixing pan of the
machine and add the remaining ingredients.

3. Put the mixing pan into the machine, close the lid,
and select the dough or pizza-dough setting.

4. After 10 minutes, check the consistency of the
dough and scrape the sides of the mixing pan with
a flexible spatula if necessary. The dough should
already be well formed. If it sticks to the pan and is
very soft, add 1¼ tablespoons (10 g) of flour. If the
dough tears and can't be formed into a nice, smooth
ball, add 2 teaspoons (10 ml) of water.

5. When the dough is ready, take it out of the
mixing pan and divide it into four pieces. On a
smooth work surface dusted with flour, spread out
one piece of the dough so that it forms a rectangle,
fold it toward you, and press the seam together. Roll
the piece of dough out slightly, leaving the seam
on the bottom. Repeat this process with the other
three pieces of dough and let them rise on a baking
sheet in a draft-free spot for about 30 minutes

6. To shape the baguettes, cut each piece of dough
on the top with scissors, making sure you don't go
all the way to the end. Then, without opening the
scissors, bend the dough to the side, alternating left
and right.

7. Preheat your oven to 425°F for 10 minutes.

8. Put the baguettes in the oven. Then pour a bit of
boiling water into a dripping pan, put the pan in the
oven, and immediately close the oven door to keep
the steam inside. Steam is the secret to baking bread
with a golden crust. Bake for 20 minutes.

9. Take the baguettes out when they're golden.

Poolish

Poolish is a type of fermentation starter that allows bread
to develop over the course of a few hours before mixing
and baking. Breads made with a poolish often have a better
aroma, texture, and flavor than "quick" breads. They also
tend to keep better.

Dark Bread

(Pain noir)

RECIPE MAKES 1 26-OUNCE (750 G) LOAF
BREAD MACHINE SETTING: WHOLE GRAIN OR
  QUICK WHOLE GRAIN

1 to 1¼ cups (260-285 ml) water: adjust according to
  machine (see Hydration Rate box, page 12)

1¼ cups (270 g) unbleached light whole-wheat flour

½ cup (100 g) rye flour

⅓ cup (80 g) whole-wheat or dark whole-wheat flour

2½ teaspoons (8 g) dehydrated yeast (also known as
  fermentable wheat yeast; sold at natural-food stores)
  or 1 teaspoon (4 g) instant baker's yeast (sold at
  supermarkets)

1½ teaspoons (6 g) salt

3 tablespoons (60 g) molasses

3 tablespoons caraway seeds

1 tablespoon fennel seeds

1 teaspoon soluble instant coffee

2 teaspoons unsweetened powdered cocoa

1. Put all of the ingredients into the mixing
pan of the machine. Make sure that the salt
doesn't touch the baker's yeast (if it does, it may
deactivate the yeast).

2. Put the mixing pan into the machine, close the
lid, and select the whole-grain or quick whole-
grain setting.

3. After 10 minutes, check the consistency of the
dough. Scrape the sides of the pan with a flexible
spatula if necessary. The dough should already be
well formed. If it sticks to the walls of the pan and
is very moist, add 1¼ tablespoons (10 g) of flour.
If the dough tears and can't be formed into a nice,
smooth ball, add 2 teaspoons (10 ml) of water.

4. When the machine is done and the baking is
complete, take the pan out of the machine. Remove
the bread from the pan and let it cool on a rack.

Hand Kneading

*The recipes in this book that are made with bread
machines can also be prepared entirely by hand. Just follow
the instructions for making Handmade White Bread on
page 10, adjusting water quantities as needed.*

Garlic and Olive Oil Bread

(Pain á l'ail et á l'huile d'olive)

RECIPE MAKES 1 26-OUNCE (750 G) LOAF
BREAD MACHINE SETTING: WHITE, BASIC, OR FRENCH

1 cup (250-270 ml) water: adjust according to machine (see Hydration Rate box, page 12)

3 tablespoons olive oil

1½ cups (350 g) high-gluten wheat flour

¾ cup (100 g) spelt flour

2½ teaspoons (8 g) dehydrated yeast (also known as fermentable wheat yeast; sold at natural-food stores) or 1 teaspoon (4 g) instant baker's yeast (sold at supermarkets)

1½ teaspoons (6 g) salt

1 teaspoon sugar

1 teaspoon lemon juice

3 cloves garlic, minced

1. Put all of the ingredients into the mixing pan of the machine. Make sure that the salt doesn't touch the baker's yeast (if it does, it may deactivate the yeast).

2. Put the mixing pan into the machine, close the lid, and select the white bread, basic, or French bread setting.

3. After 10 minutes, check the consistency of the dough and scrape the sides of the pan with a flexible spatula if necessary. The dough should already be well formed. If it sticks to the walls of the pan and is very soft, add 1¼ tablespoons (10 g) of flour. If the dough tears and can't be formed into a nice, smooth ball, add 2 teaspoons (10 ml) of water.

4. When the machine is done and the baking is complete, remove the pan from the machine. Take the bread out of the pan and let it cool on a rack.

Tip

If you have dry, leftover bread, you can do as the Catalans do and make pa amb tomàquet, or bread with tomato. Rub the leftover bread with a tomato, add a trickle of olive oil, and a pinch of salt. Delicious!

Hand Kneading

The recipes in this book that are made with bread machines can also be prepared entirely by hand. Just follow the instructions for making Handmade White Bread on page 10, adjusting water quantities as needed.

Bread with Dried Fruits
(Pain aux fruits secs)

RECIPE MAKES 1 26-OUNCE (750 G) LOAF
BREAD MACHINE SETTING: DOUGH
PREP TIME (NOT COUNTING MACHINE KNEADING AND RISING):
    20 MINUTES
SET ASIDE: 30 MINUTES
BAKING TIME: 35 TO 40 MINUTES

1 cup (240-260 ml) water: adjust according to machine
    (see Hydration Rate box, page 12)

2½ tablespoons (40 ml) milk

2¾ cups (340 g) unbleached light whole-wheat flour

¾ cup (80 g) whole rye flower

¼ cup (30 g) chestnut flour

2½ teaspoons (8 g) dehydrated yeast (also known as
    fermentable wheat yeast; sold at natural-food stores)
    or 1 teaspoon (4 g) of instant baker's yeast (sold at
    supermarkets)

1½ (6 g) teaspoons salt

1 tablespoon (15 g) butter

2 teaspoons brown sugar

3 tablespoons (20 grams) hazelnuts, almonds, or raisins

4 tablespoons granola or muesli

1. Put all of the ingredients except for the dried
fruits into the mixing pan of the machine, making
sure that the salt doesn't touch the baker's yeast
(if it does, it may deactivate the yeast).

2. Put the mixing pan into the machine, close the lid,
and select the dough setting.

3. After 10 minutes, check the consistency of the
dough and scrape the sides of the pan with a flexible
spatula, if necessary. The dough should already be
well formed. If it sticks to the sides of the pan and is
very soft, add 1¼ tablespoons (10 g) of flour. If the
dough tears and can't be formed into a nice, smooth
ball, add 2 teaspoons (10 ml) of water.

4. When the machine beeps, add the dried fruits.

5. When the machine is done, take out the dough
and place it on a smooth work surface dusted with
flour. Form three large sausages with the dough,
braid them loosely to allow for expansion, and roll
the resulting braid so that it looks like a cinnamon
roll. Let it rise for 30 minutes on a baking sheet in a
draft-free spot.

6. Preheat your oven to 425°F for 10 minutes.

7. Put the dough in the oven. Then pour a bit of
boiling water into a dripping pan, put the pan in the
oven, and immediately close the oven door to keep
the steam inside. Steam is the secret to baking bread
with a golden crust. Bake for 35 to 40 minutes.

8. Take the bread out when it's fully baked. Let it
cool on a rack before eating.

Tip

*For this high-energy bread, you can use a store-bought
trail mix if you'd like. Just don't use one with peanuts as
they'll make the bread bitter.*

Brioche Bread with Honey and Salted Butter

(Pain brioché miel et beurre salé)

RECIPE MAKES 1 26-OUNCE (750 G) LOAF
BREAD MACHINE SETTING: DOUGH
PREP TIME (NOT COUNTING MACHINE KNEADING AND RISING):
   15 MINUTES
SET ASIDE: 30 MINUTES
BAKING TIME: 40 MINUTES

1 cup (240–270 ml) liquid (50% water, 50% milk): adjust
   according to machine (see Hydration Rate box, page 12)

1 pound all-purpose or high-gluten wheat flour

2½ teaspoons (8 g) dehydrated yeast (also known as
   fermentable wheat yeast; sold at natural-food stores)
   or 1 teaspoon (4 g) instant baker's yeast
   (sold at supermarkets)

1 teaspoon (4 g) salt

3 tablespoons (40 g) salted butter

2 tablespoons (40 g) honey

1 teaspoon lemon juice

1. Put all of the ingredients into the mixing
pan of the machine, making sure that the salt
doesn't touch the baker's yeast (if it does, it may
deactivate the yeast).

2. Put the mixing pan into the machine, close the lid,
and select the dough setting.

3. After 10 minutes, check the consistency of the
dough and scrape the sides of the pan with a flexible
spatula, if necessary. The dough should already be
well formed. If it sticks to the sides of the pan and is
very soft, add 1¼ tablespoons (10 g) of flour. If the
dough tears and can't be formed into a nice, smooth
ball, add 2 teaspoons (10 ml) of water.

4. When the machine is done, take out the dough
and place it on a work surface dusted with flour.
Make three large sausages with the dough and
braid them together loosely for expansion. Let the
dough rise for 30 minutes on a baking sheet in a
draft-free spot.

5. Preheat your oven to 425°F for 10 minutes.

6. Put the dough in the oven. Then pour a bit of
boiling water into a dripping pan, put the pan in the
oven, and immediately close the oven door to keep
the steam inside. Steam is the secret to baking bread
with a golden crust. Bake for 30 to 40 minutes.

7. Take out the bread when it's thoroughly baked.
Let it cool on a rack.

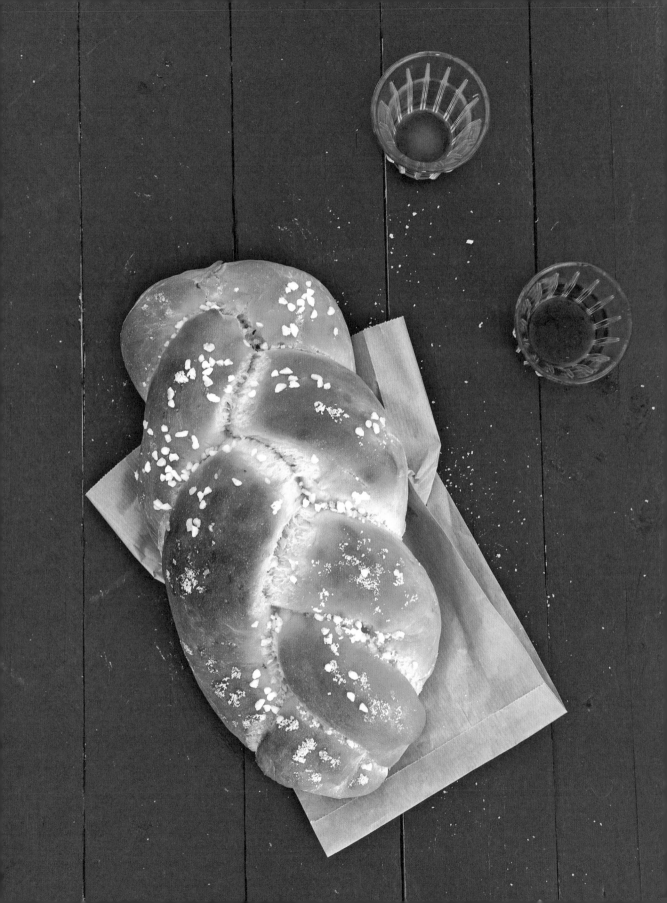

Dinner Rolls
(Pains au lait du goûter)

RECIPE MAKES 10 ROLLS
MACHINE SETTING: DOUGH
PREP TIME (NOT COUNTING MACHINE KNEADING AND RISING):
** 20 MINUTES**
BAKING TIME: 20 MINUTES

1 cup (210–230 ml) lukewarm milk: adjust according to machine (see Hydration Rate box, page 12)

2¾ cups (350 g) all-purpose or high-gluten wheat flour

2 teaspoons (6 g) dehydrated yeast (also known as fermentable wheat yeast; sold at natural-food stores) or 1 teaspoon (4 g) instant baker's yeast (sold at supermarkets)

1 teaspoon (3 g) salt

2 teaspoons (10 g) butter

1 teaspoon sugar

Milk

1. Put all of the ingredients into the mixing pan of the machine, making sure that the salt doesn't touch the baker's yeast (if it does, it may deactivate it).

2. Put the mixing pan into the machine, close the lid, and select the dough setting.

3. After 10 minutes, check the consistency of the dough and scrape the sides of the pan with a flexible spatula, if necessary. The dough should already be well formed. If it sticks to the sides of the pan and is very soft, add 1¼ tablespoons (10 g) of flour. If the dough tears and can't be formed into a nice, smooth ball, add 2 teaspoons (10 ml) of water.

4. When the machine is done, take out the dough and divide it into 10 small balls of about 2 ounces (60 g) each. On a smooth, well-floured work surface, arrange one of the balls into a rectangle. Fold it in two by turning it back toward you and press the edges together. Repeat this step again. Then roll the dough slightly to give it a cylindrical shape. Do the same with the other balls and let them rise for 20 minutes on a baking sheet in a draft-free spot.

5. Brush the balls with a little milk mixed with water.

6. Preheat your oven to 425°F for 10 minutes, and then turn the temperature down to 400°F. Bake the rolls for 20 minutes. Keep an eye on them as they bake and take them out when they're golden. Let them cool on a rack before eating.

Melba Toast
(Biscottes)

RECIPE MAKES 21 OUNCES (600 G) OF MELBA TOAST
BREAD MACHINE SETTING: WHITE OR BASIC
BAKING TIME: 15 MINUTES
DRYING TIME: 24 HOURS

¾ cup (190-210 ml) milk: adjust according to machine
(see Hydration Rage box, page 12)

⅓ cup (80–90 ml) water: adjust according to machine
(see Hydration Rate box, page 12)

1 lb (450 g) high-gluten wheat flour

2½ teaspoons (8 g) dehydrated yeast (also known as fermentable wheat yeast; sold at natural-food stores) or 1
teaspoon (8 g) instant baker's yeast (sold at supermarkets)

1½ teaspoons (6 g) salt

3 tablespoons (40 g) butter

3½ teaspoons (15 g) sugar

1. Put all of the ingredients into the pan of the
machine, making sure that the salt doesn't touch
the baker's yeast (if it does, it might deactivate
the yeast).

2. Put the mixing pan into the machine, close the lid,
and select the white or basic setting.

3. After 10 minutes, check the consistency of the
dough and scrape the sides of the pan with a flexible
spatula, if necessary. The dough should already be
well formed. If it sticks to the sides of the pan and is
very soft, add 1¼ tablespoons (10 g) of flour. If the
dough tears and can't be formed into a nice, smooth
ball, add 2 teaspoons (10 ml) of water.

4. When the machine is done, remove the pan and
take the bread out. Let it sit and dry for 24 hours.

5. Cut the bread into slices that are ⅜ inch (1 cm)
thick. Arrange the slices on a baking sheet and let
them dry for one hour.

6. Preheat your oven to 410°F for 10 minutes.

7. Put the slices in the oven for 15 minutes, turning
them once halfway through. Keep an eye on them,
because they'll cook very quickly. Take out the slices
when they're golden on both sides.

8. Turn off the oven and let the temperature fall
below 212°F. Put the slices back into the oven and
let them dry for several hours.

Traditional Brioche

(Brioche tradition à la main)

PRECIPE MAKES 1 BRIOCHE
KNEADING TIME: 40 MINUTES
SET ASIDE: 8 TO 15 HOURS
BAKING: 30 TO 40 MINUTES

3¼ cups (400 G) fluid cake and pastry wheat flour

4 small or 3 large eggs

1 egg yolk

1 packet (8 g) traditional baker's yeast (sold at supermarkets) or 1½ tablespoons (16 g) fresh baker's yeast (from bakery)

1 teaspoon (4 g) salt

5½ tablespoons (70 g) sugar

1 teaspoon vanilla-infused sugar

1 tablespoon orange flour water

2 tablespoons lukewarm milk or water

⅔ cup (150 g) + 2 tablespoons very soft butter

1 teaspoon lemon juice

1. Rehydrate the yeast in the lukewarm milk or water for 15 minutes. Mix the flour, the sugars, the salt, the lemon juice, and the orange flower water in a bowl, and add the yeast.

2. Beat the eggs and add them to the mixture. Mix the ingredients, then knead them vigorously using the palms of your hands for at least 20 minutes. The dough should stick to your fingers and be solid. Little by little, it'll become less sticky and more elastic.

3. Add the butter, mixing it into the dough. Knead the dough again for 20 minutes. It should be lighter, more flexible, and soft. It shouldn't stick to the mixing bowl or your hands.

4. When you're finished kneading the dough, cover the mixing bowl with a dishcloth and put it in a draft-free spot (in winter, leave the mixing bowl in the warmest part of the house). Let the dough rise for 1½ hours (2 hours in winter). It should double in volume.

5. Pound the dough down with a few blows of your fists and knead it lightly for one minute. Put it into a floured mixing bowl and leave it in the refrigerator for a minimum of three hours. If possible, leave it in the refrigerator overnight.

6. Take out the dough and pound it down again.

7. To make a brioche with a head, weigh the dough and set aside a quarter of it. Form the rest of the dough into a nice ball and place it in a buttered, floured tin. With the remaining quarter, make a small ball. Lightly cut a cross on the top of the large ball and insert the small one into it so that it's wedged securely in place. Let it rise again for 1 hour (1½ hours in winter) in a draft-free spot.

8. Preheat the oven to 400°F for 10 minutes.

9. Thin the egg yolk with 2 tablespoons of butter and glaze the brioche with the mixture.

10. Put the brioche into the oven and lower the temperature to 350°F. Bake it for 30 to 40 minutes. Keep an eye on it while it bakes. If it browns too quickly, cover it with a piece of aluminum foil.

11. Stick a toothpick into the brioche. If it comes out dry, the brioche is ready.

Worth the effort

When made entirely by hand, this recipe requires energy, patience, and time—but the results are worth the trouble. Remember to set out all of the ingredients the evening before you make the brioche so that they're at room temperature.

Almond Brioche
(Brioche amandes)

RRECIPE MAKES 1 BRIOCHE
BREAD MACHINE SETTING: DOUGH
PREP TIME (NOT COUNTING MACHINE KNEADING AND RISING):
  15 MINUTES
SET ASIDE: 1 HOUR
BAKING: 30 MINUTES

⅔ cup (130-150 ml) milk: adjust according to machine
  (see Hydration Rate box, page 12)

1 tablespoon rum

2 egg yolks

2¾ cups (350 g) cake and pastry wheat flour

1 teaspoon instant baker's yeast

1 teaspoon salt

¼ cup (60 g) butter

3¼ tablespoons sugar

1 teaspoon vanilla-infused sugar
1 teaspoon lemon juice

4½ tablespoons flaked almonds + 3 tablespoons for
  decoration

1. Put all of the ingredients into the pan of the machine, making sure that the salt doesn't touch the baker's yeast (if it does, it may deactivate the yeast).

2. Put the mixing pan into the machine, close the lid, and select the dough setting.

3. Wait 10 minutes, then check the consistency of the dough. Scrape the sides of the pan with a flexible spatula, if necessary. The dough should already be well formed and slightly softer than standard bread dough. If it sticks to the sides of the pan, add 1¼ tablespoons (10 g) of flour. If the dough tears and can't be formed into a nice, smooth ball, add 2 teaspoons (10 ml) of water.

4. When the machine beeps, add 4½ tablespoons (30 g) of almonds.

5. When the machine is done, take out the dough and shape it into a crown with a very large hole in the middle (the hole will close up some during the rising and baking). Let the dough rise on a baking sheet in a draft-free spot for one hour at room temperature.

6. Glaze the dough with a little milk, and then sprinkle it with flaked almonds.

7. Preheat your oven to 400°F for 10 minutes. Put the dough into the oven, reduce the temperature to 350°F, and bake it for about 30 minutes. Let it cool on a rack when it's finished baking.

Variation

You can make Raisin Brioche (brioche raisins) by using the directions for the Almond Brioche. Just change the baking temperature to 350°F and use the following ingredients:

½ cup milk: adjust according to machine (see Hydration Rate box, page 12)

2 egg yolks

3 cups cake and pastry wheat flour

1 teaspoon instant baker's yeast

2 tablespoons brown sugar

2 teaspoons vanilla-infused sugar

2 tablespoons orange flower

5 tablespoons raisins

Egg yolk mixed with water

Hand Kneading

This brioche can be made entirely by hand. Just follow the instructions for making Handmade White Bread on page 10.

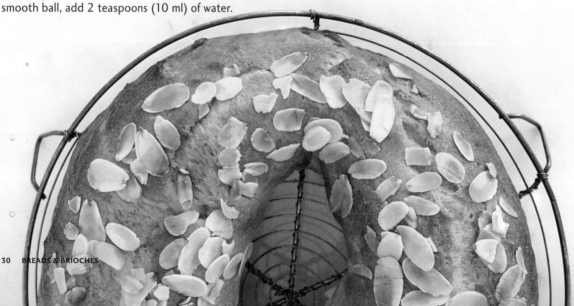

CHAPTER 2

Yogurts

plain, creamy, with fruit...

A FEW WAYS TO MAKE YOGURT

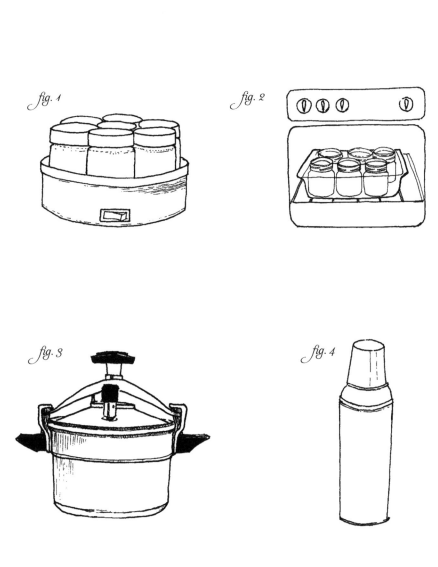

fig. 1 *fig. 2*

fig. 3 *fig. 4*

fig. 1 : yogurt maker ~ fig. 2 : in the oven ~ fig. 3 : pressure cooker ~ fig. 4 : thermos

Plain Yogurt and Cream Yogurt

(Yaourts nature et yaourts à la crème)

RECIPE MAKES 7 YOGURTS
PREP TIME: 5 MINUTES
TIME IN YOGURT MAKER: BETWEEN 6 AND 15 HOURS,
    DEPENDING ON MACHINE

1 quart whole cow's milk or soy milk

1 cup + 2 tablespoons whole cow's milk

1 cup + 2 tablespoons goat's milk at room temperature or
    slightly warmed

1 yogurt starter (a yogurt from a previous batch or a com-
    mercially made yogurt)

2 tablespoons fresh cream (optional)

1. Mix the milk with the yogurt starter.

2. To make cream yogurt, add 2 tablespoons of
fresh cream to the mixture.

3. Pour the resulting mixture into the jars. Put the
jars into the yogurt maker without their lids.

4. When the machine is done, put the lids on the
jars, and put them into the refrigerator.

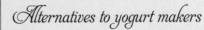

Alternatives to yogurt makers

OVEN
Preheat your oven to 100°F. Put the jars into the oven. After 2 hours, turn off the oven but don't open the door. Leave the yogurts inside without disturbing them for at least 6 hours. Then remove the yogurts and refrigerate them before serving.

PRESSURE COOKER
Boil some water in the cooker. Once the pressure is up, turn off the heat, stop the cooker, and pour out the water. Put the uncovered yogurts into the pot and immediately close it. Let the yogurts sit in the pot all night without moving them, and refrigerate them in the morning.

THERMOS
If you're really short on equipment, you can use a thermos the same way you would use a pressure cooker. The thermos will retain the heat, but the yogurt must be shaken to remove it form the thermos. Unless you eat straight from the thermos, you will only be able to make relatively thin yogurt.

Vanilla Yogurt
(Yaourts à la vanille)

RECIPE MAKES 7 YOGURTS
PREP TIME: 5 MINUTES
TIME IN YOGURT MAKER: BETWEEN 6 AND 15 HOURS,
**   DEPENDING ON MACHINE**

1 quart whole milk

1 yogurt starter (a yogurt from a previous batch or a
    commercially made yogurt)

3 teaspoons of vanilla-infused sugar

½ vanilla pod

1. Scrape the inside of the vanilla pod in order
to remove the black grains inside. Divide the
grains among the jars.

2. Mix the milk with the yogurt starter and then
add the vanilla sugar.

3. Divide the mixture among the jars and put
them into the yogurt maker without their lids.

4. When the machine is finished, put the lids on
the jars and put them in the refrigerator.

Tip
See page 35 for alternatives to a yogurt maker.

Yogurt with Homemade Apricot Jam
(Yaourts confiture d'abricots maison)

RECIPE MAKES 7 YOGURTS
PREP TIME: 15 MINUTES
COOKING TIME: 10 MINUTES
TIME IN YOGURT MAKER: BETWEEN 6 AND 15 HOURS,
   DEPENDING ON MACHINE

1 quart whole milk at room temperature

1 yogurt starter (a yogurt from a previous batch or a
   commercially made yogurt)

18 ounces very ripe apricots

2 cups sugar with pectin (for jam)

1. Wash the apricots and cut them into pieces.
Take out the kernels and set them aside.

2. To make the jam, put the apricots into boiling
water for a few minutes to remove the skin.

3. Mix the sugar with pectin and the fruit in a
large saucepan and bring the mixture to a boil.

4. Stir the mixture for 7 minutes, skim it, and
add about 10 apricot kernels. Allow the jam
to cool.

5. Put 1 generous tablespoon of jam into the
bottom of each yogurt jar.

6. In a mixing bowl, carefully mix the whole milk
and the yogurt starter. Pour the mixture into the
jars on top of the jam without stirring. Then put
the jars into the yogurt maker without their lids.

7. When the machine is finished and the yogurts
are ready, put the lids on the jars and put them
in the refrigerator.

Tip
See page 35 for alternatives to a yogurt maker.

Yogurt with Coconut & Maple Syrup

(Yaourts noix de coco et sirop d'érable)

RECIPE MAKES 7 YOGURTS
PREP TIME: 5 MINUTES
SET ASIDE: 2 HOURS
TIME IN YOGURT MAKER: BETWEEN 6 AND 15 HOURS,
    DEPENDING ON THE MACHINE

1 quart whole milk

1 yogurt starter (a yogurt from a previous batch or a
    commercially made yogurt)

½ cup grated coconut

Maple syrup for serving

1. Boil the milk along with the grated coconut. Cover the mixture and let it steep for 2 hours. When the milk has cooled thoroughly, filter it.

2. Carefully mix the filtered milk with the yogurt starter. Divide the mixture among the jars and put them into the yogurt maker without their lids.

3. When the machine is finished, put the lids on the jars and put the yogurts into the refrigerator.

4. At serving time, drizzle some maple syrup over the top each yogurt.

Variation

Make Yogurt with Honey and Roasted Almonds (yaourts au miel et amandes grillées) by splitting 5 tablespoons of honey and about 30 roasted almonds among the jars. Omit the coconut and maple syrup above.

Tip

See page 35 for alternatives to a yogurt maker.

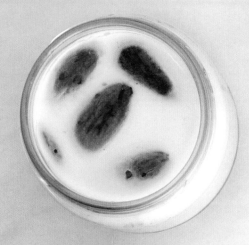

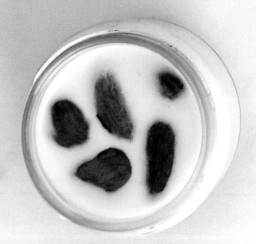

CHAPTER 3

Fresh cheeses

greek yogurt, fromage blanc, mascarpone...

MAKING CHEESE

fig. 1 : milk + whey + rennet ~ fig. 2 : placing in the container ~ fig. 3 : heating in a pot ~ fig. 4 : draining the cheese

Fromage Blanc
(Fromage blanc)

RECIPE MAKES ABOUT 14 OUNCES
PREP TIME: 10 MINUTES
TIME IN CHEESE MAKER: 10 TO 15 HOURS
DRIPPING TIME: 30 MINUTES
REFRIGERATION TIME: AT LEAST 1 HOUR

FIRST BATCH

1 quart of whole milk, preferably organic

6 to 8 drops rennet (5 drops for batches made with whey)

3½ ounces of full-fat Greek yogurt or fromage blanc, or 3½ ounces of cheese from a previous batch of fromage blanc

Large cheese drainer or small cheese drainers (see page 252)

Pyrex® container with lid and cast-iron pot or a yogurt maker with containers that fit your cheese drainers (see Note)

1. For the first batch, warm the milk to 86°F along with the Greek yogurt or store-bought fromage blanc. Make sure you mix the ingredients well and then add the 6-8 drops of rennet. After adding the rennet, stir as little as possible.

2. If you're not using a yogurt maker, fill the cast-iron pot about half-full with water and place in an oven set to 100°F. Place your cheese drainer(s) inside your glass container(s) and pour in the mixture from step 1. Put the lid on the container(s) and place the cast-iron pot in the oven or the yogurt maker for 15 hours. If you're using the cast-iron pot, remember to put the lid on the pot once the container is inside.

3. When the fromage blanc is close to the consistency shown, take the drainer(s) out of the jar(s) and let them drip in the open air for 30 minutes. Then put them on a plate and into the refrigerator. Let them continue to drip until it's time to serve.

4. For subsequent batches, warm the milk to 86°F and add 3½ ounces of fromage blanc from the preceding batch. Make sure to mix the ingredients well and then add the 5 drops of rennet. After adding the rennet, stir as little as possible. Proceed with steps 2 and 3.

5. After you've made 5 or 6 batches, start over with store-bought Greek yogurt or fromage blanc.

Note

For this recipe you need either a large glass container that fits a large cheese strainer for use in the oven, or a yogurt maker with glass jars that will fit your small cheese strainers. See page 252 for information on where to buy cheese strainers.

Faisselle
(Faisselle)

RECIPE MAKES 7 TO 10 OUNCES
PREP TIME: 5 MINUTES
SETTING TIME: 6 TO 15 HOURS
DRAINING TIME: 30 MINUTES
REFRIGERATION TIME: AT LEAST 1 HOUR

1 quart whole milk, preferably organic

5 drops rennet

3½ ounces of full-fat Greek yogurt or fromage blanc, or ½ cup whey from a previous batch of faisselle (whey is the liquid that runs out when the cheese is drained)

Large cheese drainer or small cheese drainers (see page 252)

Pyrex® container with lid and cast-iron pot or a yogurt maker with containers that fit your cheese drainers (see Notes below)

1. Warm the milk to 86°F along with the Greek yogurt, fromage blanc, or whey. Make sure to mix the ingredients well and then add the 5 drops of rennet. After adding the rennet, stir as little as possible.

2. If you're not using a yogurt maker, fill the cast-iron pot about half-full with water and place it in an oven set to 100°F. Place your cheese drainer(s) inside your glass container(s) and pour in the mixture from step 1. For this recipe, do not put the lid on your Pyrex® container or yogurt-maker container; just place them in the cast-iron pot in the oven or the yogurt maker for 10 hours. (You should put the lid on the cast-iron pot or yogurt maker.)

3. After about 10 hours, check to see if the cheese is ready. It should have a bit of whey on its surface.

4. When the cheese is close to the consistency shown, remove the drainers from the pot and let them drip for 30 minutes in the open air. Then put the drainers into the refrigerator and let them continue to drip.

Notes

For this recipe you need either a large glass container that fits a large cheese strainer for use in the oven, or a yogurt maker with glass jars that will fit your small cheese strainers. See page 252 for information on where to buy cheese strainers.

Setting times for this cheese may be shorter when the weather is hot—from 6 to ten hours. You may also need to reduce the amount of rennet used to 3 or 4 drops.

Greek Yogurt
(Yaourt á la grecque)

RECIPE MAKES 7 TO 10 OUNCES
PREP TIME: 5 MINUTES
DRIPPING TIME: AT LEAST 4 HOURS

2 cups plain, unsweetened yogurt, preferably organic

1. Put a paper coffee filter into a funnel or sieve.
Pour the yogurt into the filter and let it drip for
4 hours in the refrigerator until it thickens.

2. Serve in ramekins plain or with a little sugar, jam,
or honey.

Note
The yogurt should be eaten within 48 hours.

Petit-suisse

(Petit-suisse)

RECIPE MAKES 4 PORTIONS
PREP TIME: 10 MINUTES + TIME FOR PREPARING FAISSELLE
   (SEE PAGE 46)
REFRIGERATION TIME: AT LEAST 3 HOURS

4 pieces of faisselle, drained for a minimum of 48 hours

About ½ cup heavy cream

1. Transfer your faisselle to a mixing bowl and weigh it. Measure a third of its weight in the cream and add it to the bowl.

2. Whip everything to produce a very smooth consistency. Let the cheese firm up in the refrigerator for a few hours until serving time.

Note

Stored in a covered container in the refrigerator, this cheese can be kept for 3 to 4 days.

Tip

Line small yogurt containers or muffin tins with wax paper and spoon in the cheese before you refrigerate it. After a few hours, you can take it out and serve as shown on the facing page.

Fresh Cream Cheese
(Carré frais)

RECIPE MAKES ABOUT 14 OUNCES
PREP TIME: 10 MINUTES
TIME IN CHEESE MAKER: 15 HOURS
DRIPPING TIME: 48 HOURS

1 quart pasteurized whole milk, preferably organic

½ cup fresh, thick cream

3½ ounces of full-fat Greek yogurt or fromage blanc, or
  ½ cup whey from a previous batch of faisselle (whey is
  the liquid that runs out when the cheese is drained)

3 drops rennet

⅓ teaspoon table salt

Large cheese drainer or small cheese drainers (see page 252)

Pyrex® container with lid and cast-iron pot or a yogurt
  maker with containers that fit your cheese drainers
  (see Note below)

1. Mix the milk with the fresh cream and the Greek
yogurt, fromage blanc, or whey. Warm the mixture
to 86°F. Make sure you mix the ingredients well and
then add the 3 drops of rennet. After adding the
rennet, stir as little as possible.

2. If you're not using a yogurt maker, fill the cast-
iron pot about half-full with water and place it in
an oven set to 100°F. Place your cheese drainer(s)
inside your glass container(s) and pour in the
mixture from step 1. Put the lid on the container(s)
and place the cast-iron pot in the oven or the
yogurt maker for 15 hours. If you're using the cast-
iron pot, remember to put the lid on the pot once
the container is inside.

3. When the cheese is close to the consistency
shown, let it drip for one hour, uncovered. Then
put it in on a plate in the refrigerator and let it
continue dripping. Remove the whey at regular
intervals for at least 24 hours.

4. Pour the cheese into a mixing bowl, add the salt,
and mix with a spatula. Then spoon the mixture
into a piece of cheesecloth and set it inside a
rectangular mold, such as a small baking dish. The
mold will give the cheese its distinctive shape. Let
it sit and release whey through the cheesecloth for
another 24 hours.

Tip
*Because of its smooth texture, this cheese is easy to
spread. It's similar to American cream cheese and can
be kept in the refrigerator for one week.*

Note
*For this recipe you need either a large glass container
that fits a large cheese strainer for use in the oven, or
a yogurt maker with glass jars that will fit your small
cheese strainers. See page 252 for information on
where to buy cheese strainers.*

Mascarpone
(Mascarpone)

RECIPE MAKES ABOUT 14 OUNCES
PREP TIME: 20 MINUTES
SET ASIDE: 6 TO 10 HOURS
DRIPPING TIME: AT LEAST 12 HOURS

2 cups heavy cream, preferably organic
2 tablespoons of fresh lemon juice

1. Spoon the fresh cream into a heat-resistant container and put the container in a double-boiler. Heat it to a temperature of 176°F and then add the lemon juice. Stir the mixture continually for several minutes until it thickens.

2. Put the cream into a mixing bowl and set it aside for 6 to 10 hours. A bit of whey will form on the surface during this time.

3. Spoon the mixture into a sieve or a drainer lined with a piece of cheesecloth, and let it drip in the refrigerator for a minimum of 12 hours.

4. Transfer the mascarpone to a jar with a lid. It will keep in the refrigerator for 5 days.

Goat Cheese
(Fromage de chèvre)

RECIPE MAKES ABOUT 8 OUNCES
PREP TIME: 20 MINUTES
DRAINING TIME: 30 MINUTES + MINIMUM OF 1 HOUR IN
  THE REFRIGERATOR

½ quart goat's milk

½ quart whey from a previous batch cheese (whey is the
  liquid that runs out when the cheese is drained, and you
  can use whey from one of the other cheese recipes in
  this chapter)

1 pinch salt

Cheese drainer (see page 252)

1. Combine the goat's milk, the whey, and the salt
in a pan and slowly bring the mixture to a boil. Let it
boil for a few minutes, then remove it from the heat,
and let it cool.

2. Pour the mixture into a sieve or a drainer lined
with cheesecloth and let it drip until the whey runs
out. Press down on the cheesecloth to squeeze
out all of the whey. Then put the cheese into a
drainer—one that will give the cheese shape—
packing it slightly. Let it drip in the refrigerator until
serving time.

3. Turn the cheese out of the drainer and enjoy.

Tips
*With its pronounced taste and semi-dry texture, this
cheese is hard to resist. It should be eaten within one day.
Serve it with a side of figs or covered in honey.*

Tofu
(Tofu)

RECIPE MAKES ABOUT 7 OUNCES
PREP TIME: 10 MINUTES
SETTING TIME: 20 MINUTES

1 quart plain soymilk (unsweetened), preferably organic

2 heaping teaspoons nigari (sold at Asian-food and natural-food stores) diluted in 4 tablespoons of water

1. Bring the soymilk to a boil and add the nigari-water mixture. The milk should curdle quickly.

2. Pour the mixture into a sieve lined with very fine cheesecloth or linen. Immediately pull the four corners of the cheesecloth together and wring it to squeeze out as much whey as possible. If the cheesecloth is too hot to handle, trickle some water over it.

3. Shape the cheesecloth into a very compact ball. Put it on a wooden cutting board and put the board in the sink. Place a weight (a dish filled with water will work) on top of the ball to press out excess moisture. Let it sit for about 10 minutes. Rotate the ball and put the weight on again for 10 minutes.

4. Carefully remove the tofu from the cheesecloth. Transfer it to a container filled with water and put it in the refrigerator. Let it firm up before eating. The tofu can be kept for three days in the refrigerator. Make sure it's covered with water.

Tip

Instead of nigari, you can use two heaping teaspoons of powdered magnesium chloride (sold at pharmacies) to make this recipe.

CHAPTER 4

Pasta

tagliatelle, flavored pastas, tomato sauce...

USING THE PASTA MACHINE

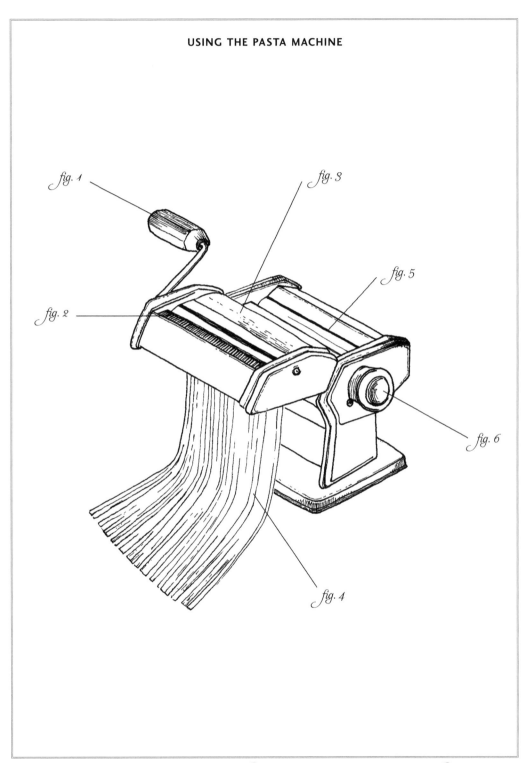

fig. 1 : crank ~ fig. 2 :tagliatelle mill ~ fig. 3 : sheet of pasta in the tagliatelle mill
fig. 4 : tagliatelle ~ fig. 5 : lasagna mill ~ fig. 6 : roller spacing knob

Fresh Pasta with Egg
(Pâtes fraîches aux oeufs)

RECIPE MAKES ABOUT 24 OUNCES (680 G) OF PASTA
PREP TIME: 30 MINUTES
SET ASIDE: 1 TO 2 HOURS

2½ cups (300 g) all-purpose flour

9½ tablespoons (100 g) pastry flour

4 medium eggs

1 tablespoon olive oil

1 pinch salt

1. Mix the all-purpose flour and the pastry flour together. Pour the mixture onto a pastry board, cutting board, or countertop. Make a hollow in the mixture and break the eggs into it.

2. Add the salt to the mixture and stir it with a fork. Gradually stir the flour-semolina mixture into the eggs.

3. Add the olive oil. Blend in the remaining flour with your fingers.

4. Work the dough with the palms of your hands until it's smooth. Shape it into a ball, cover it with plastic wrap, and set it aside for 1 to 2 hours.

ROLLING OUT THE DOUGH IN THE MACHINE:

Take about 2 ounces of dough and flatten it into a disk with the palm of your hand. Sprinkle it lightly with flour. Feed the dough into the machine, making sure the rollers are open. Fold the dough into thirds before passing it through the machine.

Repeat this step until you have a fairly regular rectangle of dough. Fold the dough in half and pass it through the machine several times, progressively tightening the rollers to produce a sheet of the desired thickness. Cut it as desired.

ROLLING THE DOUGH BY HAND:

Start by flouring your work surface thoroughly and keep it well floured as you work. Roll out the dough with a rolling pin, moving outward from the center. Work quickly so that the dough doesn't dry out. The thickness of the dough won't be consistent throughout, but the resulting pasta will retain more sauce.

Tips

• *All of the ingredients should be at room temperature before you combine them.*

• *When rolling out the dough, always work with small quantities; wrap up the rest in a plastic bag so that it doesn't dry out.*

• *Keep a dough cutter on hand for cutting off pasta pieces.*

• *If you can find imported 00 flour from Europe, it can be directly substituted for both flours in this recipe.*

Tagliatelle
(Tagliatelle)

1. Dry the sheets of fresh dough (page 62) for 10 minutes on a clean dishtowel. Make sure the towel is sprinkled with flour so that the dough doesn't stick.

2. Roll up a sheet of the dough and cut it into slices that are about ⅜ inch (1 cm) thick. Then unroll the dough and put the slices on a clean dishtowel. Put the towel with the pasta on a baking sheet or other sturdy surface and cover it. Cook within 2 days.

Other Pastas
(Les autres formes)

• Use 2 ounces of fresh dough (page 62) to make 5 x 16-inch sheets for lasagna. You can also cut these sheets down further with a pastry wheel as desired.

• To make pappardelle and tagliolini, follow the instructions for tagliatelle (at left), but cut the dough into 1-inch sections.

• If you have leftover bits of dough, you can make maltagliati. This pasta is cut randomly, often with a pastry wheel.

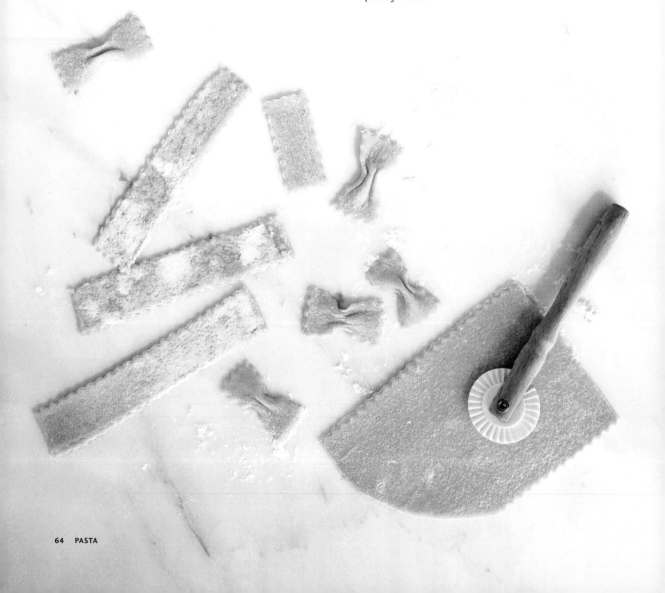

Flavored Pastas
(Les pâtes parfumées)

Spinach

RECIPE MAKES ABOUT 12 OUNCES OF PASTA
PREP TIME: 30 MINUTES
SET ASIDE: 1 TO 2 HOURS

2 cups (220 g) + 6½ tablespoons (80 g) all-purpose flour

1 cup spinach, cooked, drained, and chopped

1 egg

1 egg yolk

1 teaspoon olive oil

1 pinch salt

1. Pour the flour onto your work surface. Make a hollow in the flour and pour in the beaten eggs. Add the salt and mix with a fork.

2. Add the spinach and the olive oil, using your fingers to mix them with the flour.

3. Work the dough with the palms of your hands until it's smooth, then shape it into a ball. Wrap the dough in plastic wrap and set it aside for 1 to 2 hours.

Rosemary

RECIPE MAKES ABOUT 9 OUNCES OF PASTA
PREP TIME: 10 MINUTES
SET ASIDE: 1 TO 2 HOURS

1¼ cups (150 g) all-purpose flour

⅓ cup (50 g) pastry flour

1 tablespoon fresh rosemary, chopped

2 eggs

1 teaspoon olive oil

1 pinch salt

1. Mix the flour and the pastry flour together, and then pour the mixture onto your work surface. Make a hollow in the mixture, and break the eggs into it.

2. Add the salt and the rosemary. Stir the mixture with a fork. Then add the olive oil, working it into the flour with your fingers. Follow step 3 for Spinach Pasta.

Tomato

RECIPE MAKES ABOUT 14 OUNCES OF PASTA
PREP TIME: 30 MINUTES
SET ASIDE: 1 TO 2 HOURS

1¾ cups (220 g) all-purpose flour

½ cup (80 g) pastry flour

2½ tablespoons puréed dried tomatoes in oil

2 eggs

1 egg yolk

1. Mix the flour and the pastry flour together, and then pour the mixture onto your work surface. Make a hollow in the mixture, and add the eggs and egg yolk.

2. Mix with a fork, and then stir in the dried tomato purée. Follow step 3 for Spinach Pasta.

Cuttlefish Ink

RECIPE MAKES ABOUT 12 OUNCES OF PASTA
PREP TIME: 30 MINUTES
SET ASIDE: 1 TO 2 HOURS

2½ cups (300 g) all-purpose flour

1 teaspoon cuttlefish ink

2 tablespoons hot water

2 eggs

1 egg white

1 teaspoon of olive oil

1. Thin the cuttlefish ink in the hot water. Beat the eggs and the egg white, and add them to cuttlefish ink.

2. Pour the flour onto your work surface. Make a hollow in the flour and pour the cuttlefish ink mixture into it. Stir with a fork. Then add the olive oil, using your fingers to mix it with the flour.

3. Work the dough with the palms of your hands until it's smooth, then shape it into a ball. Wrap the dough in plastic wrap and set it aside for 1 to 2 hours.

Cooking Fresh Pasta
(La cuisson des pâtes)

SERVES 4 PEOPLE
PREP TIME: 2 MINUTES
COOKING TIME: 2-4 MINUTES

4 quarts water

2 tablespoons of salt

12 to 14 ounces of pasta

1. Fill a large pot with cold water, cover it, and bring it to a boil over high heat. Add the salt as soon as the water boils, and then pour in the pasta.

2. Stir the pasta frequently with a wooden spoon. The water should be kept at a boil.

3. After 2-4 minutes, drain the pasta. Toss with sauce or olive oil immediately to keep the pasta from sticking together, or see tip below.

Tip

Put the cooked pasta back onto the heat for 1 minute, mixing it with your sauce and a couple of spoonfuls of the water in which it was cooked. This allows the pasta to absorb the sauce more effectively.

Tomato Sauce
(Sauce tomate)

RECIPE MAKES 2 14-OUNCE BOTTLES
PREP TIME: 20 MINUTES
COOKING TIME: 50 MINUTES

2 cans (14 ounces each) peeled tomatoes, chopped

3 tablespoons olive oil

2 to 3 cloves garlic, peeled and minced

Leaves from a few stems of basil

Sugar

Salt

Pepper

1. Heat the olive oil over low heat in a saucepan or a frying pan, then add the garlic. Let the mixture cook over low heat for a few minutes. The garlic should soften, but not brown at all.

2. Add the tomatoes and simmer uncovered for 30 to 45 minutes. The sauce should cook down and thicken during this time.

3. Add the basil, then give the sauce a taste. Add a bit of salt, pepper, or sugar as needed

4. Eat the sauce immediately or put it into bottles and store in the fridge for a few days.

Smoother and Richer Sauces

• *For a smoother consistency, you can run the cooked sauce through a food mill or blender. If you use a blender, blend it briefly—you don't want to turn the sauce into a purée.*

• *To make extra-rich sauce, add 3 to 4 teaspoons of butter at the end of the cooking process.*

Using Fresh Tomatoes

Select tomatoes that are very ripe and tasty! You can leave the skin on, or you can briefly dunk them in boiling water and peel off the skins before adding them to the sauce.

Pesto

(Pesto)

RECIPE MAKES 8-OUNCES OF PESTO
PREP TIME: 15 MINUTES
COOKING TIME: 3 MINUTES

4 bunches basil

2 tablespoons pine nuts

5 tablespoons extra-virgin olive oil

4 tablespoons freshly grated Parmesan cheese

2 cloves garlic

Salt

1. Wash, drain, and pick the leaves from the basil.

2. Roast the pine nuts in a frying pan over low heat until slightly brown.

3. Mix the basil, pine nuts, olive oil, and garlic together with a morter and pestle. Add the Parmesan cheese and mix with a spoon or fork instead of the pestle. Give the mixture a taste, and add some salt if necessary. Thin it with additional extra-virgin olive oil if desired.

4. It's best if you can use the pesto immediately, but you can store it in a container in the fridge for a day or two.

CHAPTER 5

Bouillons & condiments

sauces, chutneys, infusions...

MAKING BOUILLON

fig. 1 : meats + vegetables + water ~ fig. 2 : boiling in a stock pot ~ fig. 3 : straining

Fresh Butter

(Faire son beurre)

RECIPE MAKES 4½ OUNCES
PREP TIME: 15 MINUTES

1¾ cups fresh, heavy cream (at least 35% fat content)
    without additives, preservatives, or thickeners

Electric mixer

Drainer or fine sieve

Large jar with lid

Small ceramic pots or waxed paper (for storing
    the butter)

1. Take the cream out of the refrigerator 30 minutes before use and put it in a large mixing bowl. Beat it with an electric mixer on a high speed until it becomes very firm.

2. When the cream begins to yellow, lower the speed on the mixer. Stop mixing when small yellow specks form and a sort of whey (buttermilk) appears.

3. Pour the pieces of butter into a drainer or very fine sieve, but do not press or pack them tightly. Let them drain, and then pour them into a large jar.

4. Add cold water and two or three ice cubes until the jar is three-quarters full. Put the lid on the jar and shake it vigorously for two to three minutes.

5. Pour the mixture into a drainer and let the cloudy liquid drain.

6. Repeat steps 4 and 5 until the liquid that runs off is clear.

7. Put the butter into a mixing bowl and mix it for four minutes with a wooden spatula or similar tool.

8. Pack the butter firmly into small ceramic pots or wrap it tightly in wax paper. The butter will keep for four to five days in the fridge. After that, it will start to turn rancid.

Note

If you don't have an electric mixer, don't worry! You can still make butter, although the alternative method takes a bit more time and effort: Put the fresh cream into a jar, seal it up, and shake it vigorously for about 25 minutes.

Salted butter

To add a bit of extra flavor to the butter, try salting it. Weigh the butter first to determine how much salt you need. Two good pinches are adequate for 4½ ounces of butter. Other flavorful options include herbs, garlic, or chili pepper. Just add them as you're mixing the butter. If you want the butter to have some color, add a pinch of turmeric or paprika.

Compound Butters
(Beurres parfumés)

Garlic and Parsley

PREP TIME: 15 MINUTES
REFRIGERATION TIME: 4 HOURS

½ cup soft butter (page 76)

2 pressed garlic cloves

2 tablespoons chopped parsley

Lemon juice

2 tablespoons roasted almonds, very finely chopped

A touch of cognac (optional)

1 sheet wax paper, 8 x 10 inches

1. Using a spatula, work the butter in a bowl until it's soft. Add the other ingredients and mix thoroughly.

2. Spread the mixture out lengthwise on the sheet of wax paper. Roll the paper tightly around the butter so that it forms a sausage-like shape and twist the ends as if you're wrapping a piece of candy.

3. Refrigerate the butter for at least four hours. To serve, unwrap the butter and cut it into slices.

Tarragon

PREP TIME: 15 MINUTES
REFRIGERATION TIME: 4 HOURS

½ cup soft butter (page 76)

½ tablespoon chopped tarragon

Lemon juice

Salt

Pepper

1 sheet wax paper, 8 x 10 inches

Prepare as for the Garlic and Parsley Butter

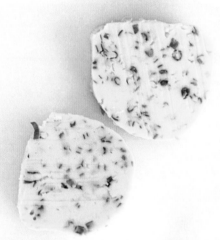

Seaweed

RECIPE SERVES 4 PEOPLE
PREP TIME: 15 MINUTES
REFRIGERATION TIME: 4 HOURS

½ cup soft butter

1 tablespoon dehydrated seaweed

1 tablespoon chopped parsley

1 chopped shallot

Salt

Pepper

Prepare as for the Garlic and Parsley Butter

Lemon and Chives

PREP TIME: 15 MINUTES
REFRIGERATION TIME: 4 HOURS

½ cup soft butter (page 76)

12 teaspoons grated lemon peel

4 tablespoons (or 1 small bunch) chopped chives

Salt

Pepper

1 sheet wax paper, 8 x 10 inches

Prepare as for the Garlic and Parsley Butter

Infused Oils
(Huiles parfumées)

Red Pepper

RECIPE MAKES ABOUT 25 OUNCES
PREP TIME: 5 MINUTES
STEEPING TIME: AT LEAST 2 WEEKS

3 cups extra-virgin olive oil

10 small dried red peppers,

4 or 5 thyme sprigs

3 oregano sprigs

10 black peppercorns

Glass bottle with stopper or cap

1. Put the peppers in the bottle first, then add the thyme, oregano, and peppercorns.

2. Fill the bottle with olive oil and cap it securely. Let the oil steep for at least two weeks.

Garlic and Basil

RECIPE MAKES ABOUT 25 OUNCES
PREP TIME: 5 MINUTES
DRYING TIME: 24 HOURS
STEEPING TIME: 2 WEEKS

3 cups extra-virgin olive oil

2 basil sprigs

3 garlic cloves, peeled

4 coriander seeds

8 black peppercorns

Glass bottle with stopper or cap

1. Dry the sprigs of basil in the sun or in the kitchen for about 24 hours, and then put them in the bottle. Add the garlic, peppercorns, and coriander seeds.

2. Fill the bottle with olive oil and cap it securely. Let the oil steep for at least two weeks.

Perfect pairings
Use your flavored oils with the following dishes:

RED PEPPER
pizza, grilled fish, green salads

GARLIC AND BASIL
tomato salad, fried steak, grilled meats

DILL
potato salad, salmon

OREGANO
pasta, pizza, grilled meats

Oregano

RECIPE MAKES ABOUT 25 OUNCES
PREP TIME: 5 MINUTES
STEEPING TIME: 10 DAYS
GLASS BOTTLE WITH STOPPER OR CAP

3 cups extra-virgin olive oil

2 or 3 fresh oregano sprigs, washed

2 tablespoons dried oregano

1. Put the sprigs of oregano in the bottle and then add the dried oregano.

2. Fill the bottle with olive oil and cap it securely. Let the oil steep for about 10 days.

Dill

RECIPE MAKES ABOUT 25 OUNCES
PREP TIME: 5 MINUTES
STEEPING TIME: 2 WEEKS

3 cups extra-virgin olive oil

12 fresh dill sprigs

10 black peppercorns

5 juniper berries

Glass bottle with stopper or cap

1. Put the peppercorns and the juniper berries in the bottle and then add the dill.

2. Fill the bottle with olive oil and cap it securely. Let the oil steep for at least two weeks.

Infused Vinegars
(Vinaigres parfumés)

Tarragon

RECIPE MAKES 1 QUART
PREP TIME: 5 MINUTES
DRYING TIME: 1 WEEK
STEEPING TIME: 3 WEEKS

5 tarragon sprigs
1 quart red wine vinegar
Glass bottle with stopper or cap

1. Dry the sprigs of tarragon for one week in a spot that's dark and free of moisture.

2. Put the dried tarragon in the bottle, add the vinegar, and cap the bottle tightly.

3. Store the vinegar in the pantry for about three weeks before using.

Honey

RECIPE MAKES 1 QUART
PREP TIME: 10 MINUTES
STEEPING TIME: 3 WEEKS

4 tablespoons honey
1 quart cider vinegar
Glass bottle

1. Pour the vinegar and the honey into a saucepan and stir. Heat the mixture over low heat for about five minutes.

2. Let the mixture cool slightly, then pour it into the bottle and seal it tightly.

3. Store the vinegar in the pantry for about three weeks before using.

Basil

RECIPE MAKES 1 QUART
PREP TIME: 5 MINUTES
STEEPING TIME: 3 WEEKS

1 basil sprig
1 quart red wine vinegar
Glass bottle with stopper or cap

1. Put the sprig of basil in the bottle, add the vinegar, and cap the bottle tightly.

2. Store the vinegar in the pantry for about three weeks before using.

Rosemary

RECIPE MAKES 1 QUART
PREP TIME: 5 MINUTES
STEEPING TIME: 3 WEEKS

1 rosemary sprig
1 quart red wine vinegar
Glass bottle with stopper or cap

1. Put the sprig of rosemary in the bottle, add the vinegar, and cap the bottle tightly

2. Store the vinegar in the pantry for about three weeks before using.

Perfect pairings
Use your flavored vinegars for cooking and in recipes:

TARRAGON
cole slaw, potato salad

ROSEMARY
grilled meats, steamed fish

BASIL
olive oil vinaigrettes

HONEY
tangy applesauce, deglazing meat

Flavored Salts
(Sels parfumés)

Mandarin

RECIPE MAKES 4 OUNCES
PREP TIME: 2 MINUTES
DRYING TIME: 24 HOURS

1 mandarin orange
2 ounces salt

1. Remove the peel from the mandarin orange and let it dry for 24 hours. You can eat the orange or use it for another recipe.

2. Once the orange peel is dry, mince finely and mix it with the salt.

Matcha

RECIPE MAKES 4 OUNCES
PREP TIME: 2 MINUTES

2 teaspoons matcha tea powder
2 ounces salt

Mix the matcha tea powder and salt together.

Coconut

RECIPE MAKES 4 OUNCES
PREP TIME: 2 MINUTES

2 ounces high-quality grated coconut
2 ounces (50 g) salt

Mix the grated coconut and the salt together.

Homemade Ketchup
(Ketchup maison)

RECIPE MAKES ABOUT TWO 9-OUNCE JARS
PREP TIME: 20 MINUTES
COOKING TIME: 1 HOUR AND 15 MINUTES

2 pounds ripe tomatoes

1 red or yellow bell pepper

1 onion

4 garlic cloves

8 tablespoons red wine vinegar

7 tablespoons sugar

Lemon peel

Lemon juice

1 heaping teaspoon salt

1 teaspoon mustard seed

½ tablespoon peppercorns

¼ tablespoon coriander seeds

½ teaspoon cloves

1 small cinnamon stick

⅜-inch piece of ginger

Cheesecloth

Glass jar with cap

1. Peel the garlic, onion, and ginger and cut them into large pieces.

2. Put the tomatoes in a mixing bowl or large pot and add boiling water.

3. As soon as the tomatoes soften, remove them from the pot. Remove the peels and chop them into small pieces.

4. Put the tomatoes, onion, garlic, and pepper in a large saucepan with half of the vinegar. Add the sugar, lemon peel, and lemon juice. Mix well to combine and cook them over medium heat for 15 minutes. Then add the rest of the vinegar and the salt.

5. Place the spices (mustard, pepper, coriander, clove, cinnamon, and ginger) on a piece of cheesecloth. Tie the gauze up with a string and put it in the saucepan with the tomato mixture. Cook the mixture for one hour over low heat until the sauce boils down and thickens. Then remove the gauze with the spices.

6. Put the ketchup in a glass jar or plastic bottle. Note: If you plan on storing the ketchup, see page 253 for instructions on sterilizing the glass jar.

Variations

• Use yellow tomatoes and a yellow bell pepper to make yellow ketchup!

• For ketchup with a noticeably sweet flavor, add a bit of extra sugar.

• Use more or less of the spices according to taste.

Mayonnaise
(Mayonnaise)

RECIPE MAKES ABOUT 10 OUNCES OF MAYONNAISE
PREP TIME: 15 MINUTES

1 egg yolk

1 teaspoon salt

1 teaspoon Dijon mustard

1¼ cups (300 ml) vegetable oil

1–2 teaspoons lemon juice

Ground pepper

1. Put the egg yolk into a large mixing bowl, add the salt and mustard, and then whisk the ingredients by hand or with a machine. Add a few drops of the vegetable oil and whisk again. Add about a third of the oil in this manner, a few drops at a time while stirring. The mixture will start to thicken.

2. At this point, you can start pouring the oil a little faster (in a thin stream) while beating the mixture. Continue until all of the oil has been added to the mixture.

3. The mayonaisse should be nice and thick, and ready for seasoning. Season it with lemon juice and pepper. It's best if you can use it the same day you make it, but it will keep overnight in the fridge.

Making use of a failed batch

Did you add the oil too fast? If so, you might have mayo that doesn't quite look like it should. But all is not lost. If you start over and make a successful batch of mayo, you can slowly fold in the failed batch as if it were more oil.

Mango Chutney
(Chutney de mangue)

RECIPE FILLS TWO 8-OUNCE JARS
PREP TIME: 15 MINUTES
SET ASIDE: 2 HOURS
COOKING TIME: 2½ HOURS

3 mangoes

1 cup brown sugar

1 pinch ground turmeric

1 teaspoon ground cinnamon

1 teaspoon fresh ginger, grated

½ teaspoon table salt

2 garlic cloves, chopped

1 large onion, finely minced

1¼ cups malt or white wine vinegar

2 sterilized jars (see page 253)

1. Peel the mangoes, remove the pits, and cut the flesh into small cubes. Put the fruit in a bowl with the brown sugar, turmeric, cinnamon, and ginger. Mix thoroughly and set aside, covered, for about two hours.

2. Put the cubes of mango into a thick-bottomed pan and add the salt, vinegar, garlic, and onion. Bring the mixture to a simmer and then cook it over low heat for about 2½ hours. The chutney will slowly thicken. Stir it occasionally to keep it from sticking to the pan.

3. Turn off the heat and let the chutney cool for about 20 minutes. Then pour it into the jars and cap them tightly. Turn the jars over to create a vacuum.

Tip

This chutney will taste even better if you let it sit for a couple of weeks. Store it in the fridge.

Orange-Date Chutney
(Chutney pomme-raisin)

RECIPE FILLS THREE 8-OUNCE JARS
PREP TIME: 10 MINUTES
COOKING TIME: 2½ HOURS

¾ cup oranges

1⅓ cup dates

2 cups apples

1 cup brown sugar

2 teaspoons fresh grated ginger

½ teaspoon table salt

1¼ cup white wine vinegar

3 sterilized jars (see page 253)

1. Peel the apple and cut it into quarters. Then remove the seeds and cut the apple quarters into thin slices. Cut the orange into small pieces and remove the white membrane. Pit the dates and cut them into small chunks.

2. Put the apple, orange, and date pieces into a thick-bottomed pan and add the brown sugar, salt, grated ginger, and vinegar.

3. Bring the ingredients to a simmer. Turn the heat to low and cook the mixture for about 2½ hours. The chutney will slowly thicken. Stir it regularly to keep it from sticking to the pan.

4. Turn off the heat and let the chutney sit for about 20 minutes. Pour it into the jars and cap them tightly. Turn the jars over to create a vacuum.

Tip
This chutney will taste even better if you let it sit for a couple of weeks. Store it in the fridge.

Apple-Raisin Chutney
(Chutney pomme-raisin)

RECIPE FILLS THREE 8-OUNCE JARS
PREP TIME: 10 MINUTES
SET ASIDE: 1 HOUR
COOKING TIME: 2½ HOURS

1 pound apples

1½ cups raisins

1 cup brown sugar

1 teaspoon fresh, grated ginger

½ teaspoon table salt

1 large onion, finely minced

1¼ cup cider vinegar

3 sterilized jars (see page 253)

1. Peel the apples and cut them into quarters. Then remove the seeds and cut the apple quarters into thin slices.

2. Put the apples and the rest of the ingredients into a bowl and set it aside for about an hour.

3. Pour the ingredients into a thick-bottomed pan, bring them to a simmer, and then cook them over low heat for about 2½ hours. The chutney will thicken slowly. Stir it regularly to keep it from sticking to the bottom of the pan.

4. Turn off the heat and let the chutney cool for about 20 minutes. Then pour it into the jars and cap them tightly. Turn the jars over to create a vacuum.

Tip
This chutney will taste even better if you let it sit for a couple of weeks. Store it in the fridge.

Onion Jam
(Confiture d'oignons)

RECIPE FILLS THREE 8-OUNCE JARS
PREP TIME: 10 MINUTES
COOKING TIME: 45 MINUTES

18 ounces onions

4 ounces grenadine syrup

4 ounces red wine

2 ounces wine vinegar

¾ cup super-fine sugar

Salt

Pepper

3 sterilized jars (see page 253)

1. Peel and mince the onions. Then cook them gently in a covered, non-stick pan for about 10 minutes.

2. Add the vinegar and the wine and then cook the ingredients down over high heat, uncovered, for five minutes. Lower the heat and add the sugar, grenadine, salt, and pepper.

3. Mix the ingredients and cook them over very low heat for about 30 minutes. Let the jam stew gently.

4. Remove the jam from the heat and let it cool slightly. Carefully transfer the jam to the jars if you plan on storing it. If you want to keep a jar out to use the same day, you do not have to worry about sterilizing the jar.

Chicken Bouillon
(Bouillon de poulet)

RECIPE MAKES ABOUT 1 QUART
PREP TIME: 5 MINUTES
COOKING TIME: 2½ HOURS

One 3-pound chicken (or the same amount of chicken
    carcass, wings, and necks)

1 onion

1 carrot, peeled and cut in half

1 leek, peeled and quartered

1 fennel bulb, cut in half

2 garlic cloves, peeled and crushed

1 bouquet garni (tied bunch of parsley, thyme, bay leaves)

2 tablespoons salt

10 black peppercorns

3 quarts cold water

Fine sieve or strainer

1. Put the chicken or the carcass (along with the
giblets if you have them) into a pot. Add the water
and gently bring the mixture to a boil.

2. Use a skimmer to remove the foam that forms
on the surface of the mixture. Add the rest of the
ingredients. Cover the mixture and let it simmer for
2½ hours.

3. Take the bouillon off the heat and set it aside for
15 minutes. Store it in the refrigerator for a couple
of days, or freeze it for later use.

Asian-inspired bouillon

If you want to make a chicken bouillon with a different
flavor profile, simmer a 3-pound chicken for 2½ hours
with the following ingredients:

1 bunch green onions

1 carrot

3½ tablespoons minced ginger

2 garlic cloves

1 lemongrass stalk, split lengthwise

Salt

Duck bouillon

Boil a 3-pound duck in a stewpot for 2½ hours with the
following ingredients:

2 onions, quartered

4 garlic cloves, peeled and crushed

1 tied bunch of thyme and dried fennel

1 star anise

Salt and pepper

Removing grease from a bouillon

Refrigerate your bouillon overnight. On the following day,
you can skim the layer of grease that has solidified on
the surface.

Beef Bouillon
(Bouillon d´agneau)

RECIPE MAKES ABOUT 1 QUART
PREP TIME: 10 MINUTES
COOKING TIME: 2½ HOURS

1 pound of beef (flank or rump)

1 carrot, peeled

1 onion stuck with 2 cloves

2 garlic cloves

1 leek cut into large pieces

1 bouquet garni (tied bunch of parsley, thyme,
   bay leaf)

1 tablespoon salt

10 black peppercorns

3 quarts cold water

Fine sieve or strainer

1. Put the meat in a pot with the water and
slowly bring it to a boil.

2. Use a skimmer to remove the foam that forms
on the surface of the water. Add a glass of cold
water to the pot and skim the mixture again.

3. Add the rest of the ingredients, cover the
pot, and simmer the bouillon for 2½ hours. Then
take the bouillon off the heat and set it aside for
15 minutes.

4. Filter the bouillon through a fine sieve or a
strainer. Store it in the refrigerator for a couple
of days, or freeze it for later use.

Tip
*To add some color to the bouillon, cut the onion in
half and brown it with a little oil in the oven or in a
coated, non-stick pan before adding it to the bouillon.*

Lamb Bouillon
(Bouillon d'agneau)

RECIPE MAKES 1 QUART
PREP TIME: 10 MINUTES
COOKING TIME: 2½ HOURS

18 ounces collar of lamb or defatted brisket

1 onion

1 carrot, peeled and cut in half

1 leek, peeled and quartered

1 fennel bulb, cut in half

1 celery stalk

1 tomato

1 tablespoon tomato concentrate

1 bouquet garni (tied bunch of thyme, parsley, mint, and cilantro)

1 tablespoon salt

10 peppercorns

2 quarts water

Fine sieve or strainer

1. Put the meat and vegetables in a pot with the salt, tomato concentrate, and bouquet garni. Add the water and bring the ingredients to a boil.

2. Use a skimmer to remove the foam that develops on the surface of the water. Add the rest of the ingredients, cover the pot, and simmer for 2½ hours.

3. Take the bouillon off the heat and set it aside for 15 minutes. Store it in the refrigerator for a couple of days, or freeze it for later use.

Tip

Lamb bouillon can be used instead of water to prepare a savory couscous.

Pork bouillon

To make pork bouillon, put 18 ounces of spare ribs or brisket in a pot with two quarts of water and bring it to a boil. Skim the foam off the surface of the water, and then add the same ingredients you used to make the lamb bouillon, except for the tomato and tomato concentrate. Add a small piece of minced ginger, 10 coriander seeds, and five tablespoons of soy sauce.

Fish Bouillon
(Bouillon de poisson)

RECIPE MAKES 1 QUART
PREP TIME: 10 MINUTES
COOKING TIME: 1 HOUR
SET ASIDE: 15 MINUTES

2 pounds fish bones (whiting, sole, or flounder)

1 shallot, peeled and chopped

1 onion, peeled and chopped

3½ ounces mushrooms, cleaned and minced

1 tablespoon sunflower oil

7 tablespoons dry white wine

1 bouquet garni (tied bunch of thyme, parsley, celery, and green section of a leek)

Sea salt

2 quarts cold water

Fine sieve or strainer

1. Rinse the fish bones thoroughly with cold water.

2. Put all of the vegetables in a pot with the oil and fry them over low heat for five minutes.

3. Add the fish bones and cook the mixture for five more minutes. Pour in the white wine and cook all of the ingredients for one minute. Add the water, the bouquet garni, and salt, and simmer, covered, for 50 minutes.

4. Take the bouillon off the heat and set it aside for 15 minutes. Filter it through a fine sieve or a strainer. Store it in the refrigerator for a couple of days, or freeze it for later use.

Fish bouillon with mussels

Put 18 ounces of brown shrimp in a pot with the bouquet garni and a quart of water. Bring the ingredients to a boil and then simmer them for 25 minutes. Take the bouillon off the heat, cover it, and set it aside for 15 minutes. Filter it through a fine sieve or a strainer. Store it in the refrigerator for a couple of days, or freeze it for later use.

Shrimp bouillon

To make pork bouillon, put 18 ounces of spare ribs or brisket in a pot with two quarts of water and bring it to a boil. Skim the foam off the surface of the water, and then add the same ingredients you used to make the lamb bouillon, except for the tomato and tomato concentrate. Add a small piece of minced ginger, 10 coriander seeds, and five tablespoons of soy sauce.

Shellfish bouillon

Soak 18 ounces of shellfish in a pot with cold water and some salt for an hour or two. Then rinse the fish thoroughly and put them in a pot with a stalk of celery, an onion, a clove of garlic, a small piece of ginger, and a little salt. Add 1½ quarts of water and bring the ingredients to a boil. Simmer for 40 minutes and then strain. Store it in the refrigerator for a couple of days, or freeze it for later use.

Vegetable Bouillon
(Bouillon de légumes)

RECIPE MAKES 1 QUART
PREP TIME: 10 MINUTES
COOKING TIME: 30 MINUTES
SET ASIDE: 10 MINUTES

2 carrots

2 onions

2 tomatoes

4 garlic cloves

2 celery stalks

3½ ounces cultivated mushrooms

1 bouquet garni (thyme, parsley, tarragon, chervil, green sections of leeks)

1 piece star anise

1 tablespoon gray sea salt

2 to 3 quarts cold water

Sterilized jar

1. Peel all of the vegetables and cut them into small cubes. Put them in a pot with the bouquet garni, star anise, salt, and water.

2. Simmer the bouillon for 30 minutes. Then take it off the heat, cover it, and set it aside for 15 minutes. Filter it through a fine sieve or a strainer. Store it in the refrigerator for a couple of days, or freeze it for later use.

Asian-inspired bouillon

Give your vegetable bouillon some extra spice by adding a small piece of minced ginger, a split stalk of lemongrass, and a few kaffir lime leaves.

Fresh Sprouts
(Graines germées)

PREP TIME: 5 MINUTES
SET ASIDE: 3 TO 5 DAYS

1 glass jar

Sterile gauze

Rubber band

1 tablespoon of dry grains or beans (quinoa and chickpeas
   both work well)

1. Put the grains or beans in the jar and add plenty
of water. Let the mixture soak for 12 hours.

2. Pour the water out and rinse the grains or beans.
Fill the jar with water again and then immediately
pour it out. Repeat this process several times,
shaking the jar when it's filled with water. When the
grains or beans are rinsed, there shouldn't be any
water in the jar; they should just be moist.

3. Cover the jar with the gauze and rubber band.
Store the jar in a dark spot at room temperature
for three to five days. Rinse the jar regularly: three
times a day, fill it with water and then pour it out.
The seeds should remain in the jar while you rinse.
Replace the gauze when you're done rinsing the
grains or beans.

4. Keep an eye on the seeds as they sprout. When
the sprouts reach the desired length, remove the
seeds from the jar. See page 110 for a couple of
ways to use fresh sprouts.

Bagels with Salmon and Sprouts

(Bagels au saumon pousses de roquette)

RECIPE SERVES 4 PEOPLE   PREP TIME: 10 MINUTES

4 sesame bagels

3½ ounces cream cheese

3½ ounces smoked salmon

1 tablespoon capers

2 tablespoons pickles

1¾ ounces fresh sprouts (page 108)

1. Cut each of the bagels in half and toast them; then chop the capers and the pickles.

2. Generously cover each bagel half with the cheese spread. Then add the capers, pickles, and smoked salmon. Top the bagels off with the sprouts.

Almond Salad with Sprouts and Seeds

(Salad aux amandes et graines variées)

RECIPE SERVES 4 PEOPLE   PREP TIME: 10 MINUTES

3⅓ ounces fresh sprouts (page 108)

3 tablespoons sunflower seeds

2 tablespoons pumpkin seeds

1¾ ounces flaked almonds

VINAIGRETTE DRESSING

2 tablespoons tarragon vinegar

1 teaspoon Dijon mustard

1 teaspoon honey

3 tablespoons extra-virgin olive oil

1. In a large bowl, mix the fresh sprouts, seeds, and almonds.

2. Mix the tarragon vinegar with the Dijon mustard, honey, and olive oil in a medium-sized bowl.

3. At serving time, spoon heaps of the almond salad onto plates and drizzle each with the dressing.

CHAPTER 6

Preserved foods

in oil, vinegar, salt...

PRESERVING VEGETABLES

fig. 1

fig. 2

fig. 3

fig. 4

fig. 5

fig. 1 : blanching ~ fig. 2 : filling the jar ~ fig. 3 : adding the salted water
fig. 4 : sealing the jar ~ fig. 5 : sterilizing

Dried Tomatoes in Oil
(Tomates séchées à l'huile)

RECIPE MAKES 21 OUNCES
PREP TIME: 15 MINUTES
COOKING TIME: 1½ HOURS

18 ounces ripe tomatoes

1 clove garlic

1 bay leaf

1 tablespoon vinegar

3 cups olive oil

Sterilized jar (page 253)

1. Rinse and dry the tomatoes. Cut them in half and remove the seeds. Cut the garlic clove into thin slices.

2. Preheat your oven to 250°F. Cook the tomatoes and garlic for 1½ hours, or until they're quite soft. Remove them from the oven and let them cool.

3. Put the tomatoes in the jar with the bay leaf. Add the vinegar and olive oil, then cap the jar tightly. Store it in the pantry, making sure that the tomatoes are always thoroughly covered with oil.

Note

The tomatoes will keep for many months before you open the jar. Once the jar is opened, store it in the fridge and use it within a few weeks.

Sun-dried tomatoes

Instead of cooking the tomatoes in the oven, try drying them in the sun—the way it's traditionally done in many Mediterranean countries. Place the quartered tomatoes on a pan and put it out in the sun, making sure that the tomatoes are out of the way. You don't want them coated in dust. Leave them in the sun for several days, turning them regularly and bringing them indoors at night to protect them from humidity.

Anchovies in Salt

(Anchois au sel)

RECIPE MAKES 2 POUNDS OF ANCHOVIES
PREP TIME: 45 MINUTES
SET ASIDE: 4 WEEKS

2¼ pounds anchovies

2¼ pounds salt

Peppercorns

Bay leaves

Cloves

Sterilized jar (page 253)

1. To prep the anchovies: Rinse them in cool water. Take one of the anchovies and place it on your work surface. To remove the skin, hold it by the tail as you scrape along its length (on both sides) with the knife. If the anchovy has a fin, pull it off along with any bones that might be attached. Then scrape the spine so that the anchovy opens up and lies flat, grasp the spine at the tail end, and pull it out. You should now have two boneless fillets. Use a knife to remove any intestines. Repeat with the rest of the anchovies and rinse them again in cool water.

2. Put the anchovies in a bowl and cover them with about a pound of salt. Mix the anchovies with the salt until they're thoroughly coated and set them aside until the following day.

3. Pour some of the remaining salt into the jar until the bottom is completely covered. Arrange the anchovies belly down and then add half of a bay leaf, six peppercorns, and two cloves. Repeat the layering process, starting again with salt, until the jar is filled.

4. Cap the jar tightly and store it in a cool, dark spot for a week.

5. Open the jar and skim off the oil that has formed on the surface. Add a little of the remaining salt and seal the jar tightly. Let it sit in a cool, dark spot for three weeks. Eat within three months.

Anchovies in Oil

(Anchois à l'huile)

RECIPE MAKES 2 POUNDS OF ANCHOVIES
PREP TIME: 45 MINUTES
SET ASIDE: 1 WEEK

2¼ pounds anchovies

2¼ pounds cooking salt

Peppercorns

Bay leaves

Cloves

Olive oil

2 sterilized jars (page 253)

1. Follow steps 1 and 2 for preparing Anchovies in Salt. Then pour some of the remaining salt into the jars until the bottoms are completely covered. Arrange the anchovies belly down and then add half of a bay leaf, six peppercorns, and two cloves. Repeat the layering process, starting again with salt, until the jars are filled.

2. Cap the jar, put a weight on top of it, and store it in a cool, dark spot for a week.

3. Remove the anchovy filets from the jar one by one and wipe them off. Put them into a sterilized jar and cover them with olive oil.

4. Close the jar tightly, put it in a large pan of water, and bring the water to a boil. Let it boil for 90 minutes and then let it cool. Repeat again for 30 minutes on the following day. Eat within six months.

Stuffed Cherry Peppers
(Petits poivrons farcis au thon)

RECIPE FILLS ONE 18-OUNCE JAR
PREP TIME: 15 MINUTES
COOKING TIME: 2 MINTES

12 ounces red cherry peppers

1 large can tuna, packed in oil

3¼ cups olive oil

1 teaspoon black peppercorns

2 bay leaves

Sterilized jar (page 253)

1. Rinse and dry the bay leaves and peppers. Cut the peppers open at the top and remove the seeds.

2. Bring a large pan of water to a boil and add the peppers. Leave them in the boiling water for two minutes and then drain.

3. Crumble the tuna with a fork. Stuff each of the small peppers with the tuna.

4. Put the peppers in the jar along with the peppercorns and bay leaves. Cover the ingredients with olive oil and seal the jar tightly. Store the jar in a dark, cool spot.

Note

The peppers will keep for 10 to 12 months.

Marinated Feta
(Feta marinée)

RECIPE FILLS ONE 18-OUNCE JAR
PREP TIME: 10 MINUTES
7 OUNCES FETA CHEESE

Recipe fills one 18-ounce jar

Prep time: 10 minutes

7 ounces feta cheese

¾ cup olive oil

1-2 teaspoons dried thyme and oregano

Sterilized jar (page 253)

1. Cut the feta into small cubes.

2. Put the feta in the jar one cube at a time, sprinkling in some herbs after every few pieces. Cover the feta with olive oil.

3. Seal the jar and store it in a cool spot (not as cool as the refrigerator—the cold temperature will cause the oil to congeal). Wait at least 10 days before eating.

Goat cheese in olive oil
(Petits chèvres)

RECIPE FILLS ONE 32-OUNCE JAR

10 small, fresh goat cheese pieces

2 sprigs thyme

1 small bay leaf

12 black peppercorns

3 cups olive oil

Sterilized jar (page 253)

1. Put the cheese pieces in the jar and mix in the thyme, bay leaf, and black peppercorns. Cover the ingredients with olive oil.

2. Seal the jar and store it in a cool spot (not as cool as the refrigerator—the cold temperature will cause the oil to congeal). Wait at least 10 days before eating.

Baby Onions in Vinegar

(Petits oignons au vinaigre)

RECIPE FILLS ONE 32-OUNCE JAR
PREP TIME: 20 MINUTES
COOKING TIME: 5 MINUTES
SET ASIDE: 2 MONTHS

1 pound baby pearl onions

2 cups white wine vinegar

1 clove

1 bay leaf

A few black peppercorns

Sterilized jar (page 253)

1. Peel the baby onions and rinse them with cold water.

2. Bring a large pot of water to a boil. Put the onions in for two minutes and then drain them.

3. Transfer the onions to the jar and add the clove, peppercorns, and bay leaf.

4. Boil the wine vinegar for three minutes. Take the pan off the burner and let it cool.

5. Add the boiled vinegar to the jar, covering the baby onions thoroughly, and then seal the jar tightly. Store the onions in a dark, cool spot for a month or two before eating.

Note

These onions are best eaten a month or two after they're made, but they will keep for up to a year.

Cornichons with Tarragon
(Cornichons vinaigre-estragon)

RECIPE FILLS THREE 18-OUNCE JARS
PREP TIME: 25 MINUTES
SET ASIDE: 6 TO 8 WEEKS

2¼ pounds small pickling cucumbers

1 quart white vinegar

4 shallots

10 tarragon sprigs, fresh or dried

15 black peppercorns

15 coriander seeds

1 cup salt

3 sterilized jars (page 253)

1. Cut the stems off of each of the cucumbers and rub them with a clean dish towel to remove the fuzz.

2. Put the cucumbers in a large mixing bowl and add the salt. Mix the salt and the cucumbers thoroughly and set them aside for one night. The salt will draw much of the water from the cucumbers.

3. On the following day, drain the cucumbers and wipe them with a clean dish towel.

4. Divide the cucumbers among the three jars and then add the shallots, tarragon, peppercorns, coriander seeds, and vinegar, distributing them among the jars.

5. Seal the jars tightly and store them in a dark spot. Wait six to eight weeks before eating.

Sweet-and-Sour Pickles
(Cornichons à l'aigre-doux)

RECIPE FILLS ONE 22-OUNCE JAR
PREP TIME: 15 MINUTES
COOKING TIME: 40 MINUTES
SET ASIDE: 1 MONTH

18 ounces large pickling cucumbers

½ cup white wine vinegar

2½ tablespoons water

4 teaspoons super-fine sugar

½ carrot, sliced

Dill sprigs

1 white onion, minced

5 black peppercorns

5 coriander seeds

2 teaspoons salt

Sterilized jar (page 253)

1. Mix the vinegar, water, salt, and sugar in a thick-bottomed pan. Bring the mixture to a boil and take it off the heat as soon as the first bubbles appear. Let the mixture cool until it's lukewarm and then pour it in the jar with the cucumbers.

2. Seal the jar, put it in a large pot of water, and bring the water to a boil. Let it simmer for about 30 minutes. Then allow the jar to cool in the pan.

3. Store the jar in a cool, dark spot for about a month before opening.

Pickled Vegetables
(Pickles de petits légumes)

RECIPE FILLS ONE 32-OUNCE JAR
PREP TIME: 20 MINUTES
COOKING TIME: 10 MINUTES
SET ASIDE: 2 WEEKS

7 ounces carrots

7 ounces baby onions

7 ounces cauliflower florets

4 ounces red bell pepper

2½ cups malt vinegar

1 teaspoon powdered mustard

1 teaspoon fresh ginger, grated

1 teaspoon table salt

Sterilized jar (page 253)

1. Peel the baby onions and rinse them with cold water. Then wash the carrots, red pepper, and cauliflower florets and let them drain for a minute. Cut the carrots and red pepper into small slices.

2. Boil the onions, carrots, red pepper, and cauliflower in a large pot of salted water for two minutes and then drain. Put the vegetables into the jar.

3. Pour the malt vinegar into a pot and add the mustard and ginger. Bring the mixture to a boil and let it cook for about three minutes. Then remove the pot from the heat and filter the vinegar.

4. Pour the vinegar into the jar with the vegetables and then seal the jar tightly. Store it in a dark, cool place for at least two weeks before eating.

Note
The vegetables will keep for several months.

Green Olives
(Olives vertes)

RECIPE MAKES 20 OUNCES
PREP TIME: 45 MINUTES
COOKING TIME: 5 MINUTES
STEEPING TIME: 5 WEEKS

18 ounces fresh green olives

About 1¾ cups of salt

1-quart Mason jar

2 sterilized jars (page 253)

1. Rinse the olives in cool water and then let them drain. Put them in the Mason jar and add water until the olives are covered. Then add two tablespoons of salt and cover. Change the water and the salt every day for the next 10 days.

2. Fill a pot with one quart of water and add ⅓ cup of salt. Boil it for five minutes. Remove it from the heat and let it cool.

3. Transfer the olives into the sterilized jars, leaving the water behind. Cover the olives with the fresh salt water from step 2. Make sure the olives are completely covered with the salt water.

4. Cap the jars and let the olives steep for about four weeks.

Tip

For olives with extra flavor, add one clove of peeled garlic or a few sprigs of fennel to the recipe above.

Salted Capers
(Câpres au sel)

RECIPE MAKES 18 OUNCES
PREP TIME: 45 MINUTES
SET ASIDE: 1 NIGHT

10 ounces fresh capers

1 cup salt

5 peppercorns

Sterilized jar (page 253)

1. Rinse the capers in cool water and then let them drain. Put them in a bowl and mix them with the salt until they're thoroughly coated. Set them aside until the following day.

2. Pour a thin layer of salt into the bottom of the jar. Add the capers and peppercorns. Seal the jar tightly and store it in a cool, dark spot.

Tip

Rinse the capers in cool water before eating them. Once the jar is opened, it should be stored in the refrigerator.

Preserving with salt
This type of mixture should be used a month or two after it's made, although it can keep for up to a year.

Lemons Pickled in Salt
(Citrons confits au sel)

RECIPE FILLS ONE 18-OUNCE JAR
PREP TIME: 10 MINUTES
SET ASIDE: 1 MONTH

10 lemons
1¾ cups salt
Sterilized jar (page 253)

1. Wash the lemons in cool water and dry them. Put them in a bowl and add cold water to cover, along with three or four tablespoons of salt. Set the lemons aside, covered, for six days, changing the salted water every day.

2. Slice the lemons into quarters. Sprinkle one good pinch of salt on each quarter.

3. Put the lemons in the jar, packing them in tightly, and add one tablespoon of salt. Cap the jar and let the lemons steep for a month at room temperature before refrigerating.

Note

The lemons will keep for several months in the fridge.

Preserved Peas and Carrots

(Petits pois-carottes au naturel)

RECIPE FILLS TWO 18-OUNCE JARS
PREP TIME: 15 MINUTES
COOKING TIME: 1¼ HOURS

2 pounds peas, shelled

10 ounces carrots, peeled and sliced

¾ teaspoon salt per quart of water

1 pinch super-fine sugar

2 sterilized jars (page 253)

1. Fill a large pot with water, adding ¾ teaspoon of salt for every quart of water.

2. Bring the water to a boil and add the peas. Blanch them for three minutes and drain them. Rinse them in cool water and let them drain again. Do the same with the carrots, but this time reserve the salted cooking water. Let it cool a bit, but not all the way to room temperature.

3. Layer the peas in the jars and then add the carrots. Pour the salted water over the vegetables, leaving about an inch of space at the top of each jar. Add the super-fine sugar to each jar.

4. Seal the jars tightly and put them in a large pot. Fill the pot with water until the jars are covered and bring the water to a boil. Boil the jars for one hour and then let them cool in the pot. Store them in a dark, cool spot.

Note

Vegetable preserves can be kept for a year, but if you notice mold forming on the surface of a jar, you should throw it away! Mold most often occurs when the jar wasn't sealed or sterilized properly.

Preserved Asparagus

(Asperges au naturel)

RECIPE FILLS TWO 14-OUNCE JARS
PREP TIME: 15 MINUTES
COOKING TIME: 1½ HOURS

28 ounces white asparagus
¾ teaspoon salt per quart of water
Kitchen twine
2 sterilized jars (page 253)

1. Peel the asparagus, rinse them in cool water, and let them drain. Then cut the bottoms off of the asparagus so that they'll fit upright in the jars. (Their tops will need to be at least ½ inch lower than the lids of the jars.) Use kitchen twine to tie the asparagus into bundles of 10.

2. Bring a large pot of salted water to a boil, add the asparagus, and blanch them for five minutes. Remove them with tongs and place them in a colander, rinse them in cool water, and let them drain.

3. Put the asparagus in the jars so that their spears are pointing upward. Pour the salted water into the jars, leaving about an inch of space at the top of each.

4. Seal the jars tightly and put them in a large pot. Fill the pot with water until the jars are covered, and bring the water to a boil. Boil the jars for one hour and then let them cool in the pot. Repeat this process on the following day, boiling the jars for 30 minutes. Then store them in a dark, cool spot.

Preserved Green Beans
(Haricots verts au naturel)

RECIPE FILLS TWO 14-OUNCES JARS
PREP TIME: 15 MINUTES
COOKING TIME: 1¼ HOURS

2 pounds green beans
¾ teaspoon salt per quart of water
2 sterilized jars (page 253)

1. Cut off the ends of the beans, remove any strings, and then rinse the beans in cool water.

2. Bring a large pot of salted water to a boil and add the beans. Blanch them for three minutes and let them drain. Then rinse them in cool water and let them drain again.

3. Put the beans in the jars and add the salted water, leaving about an inch of space at the top of each jar.

4. Seal the jars tightly and put them in a large pot. Fill the pot with water until the jars are covered and bring the water to a boil. Boil the jars for 75 minutes and then let them cool in the pot. Store the jars in a dark, cool spot.

Ratatouille
(Ratatouille)

RECIPE MAKES 2 QUARTS
PREP TIME: 30 MINUTES
COOKING TIME: 2 HOURS

2 pounds tomatoes

18 ounces zucchini, sliced

18 ounces eggplant, sliced

18 ounces bell peppers, thinly sliced

18 ounces onions, minced

5 small garlic cloves, chopped

Leaves from a sprig of thyme

1 parsley bunch

1 handful basil leaves

Olive oil

Salt

Ground pepper

2 sterilized jars (page 253)

1. Heat up a large pot of water to a near boil.
Add the tomatoes and a couple of pinches of salt.
Blanch them for three minutes, drain them, and rinse
them in cool water. Then remove the skins, cut the
tomatoes into halves, and remove the seeds.

2. Heat two tablespoons of olive oil in a pan and
add the tomatoes, garlic, onion, basil, and thyme.
Simmer the ingredients for about 15 minutes and
then transfer them to a container and set them
aside.

3. Heat a tablespoon of oil in the pan and cook
the eggplant over medium-low heat for about 15
minutes, turning the slices regularly and salting them
lightly. Remove the slices from the pan, put them
in a container, and set them aside. Then cook the
zucchini in the pan for about 10 minutes, turning
and salting the slices regularly. Do the same with the
bell pepper.

4. Put all of the vegetables in a pot with the tomato
sauce, add a generous amount of pepper, and cook
the ingredients over low heat for 35 minutes.

5. Pour the ratatouille into the jars, leaving about an
inch of space at the top of each jar.

6. Seal the jars tightly and put them in a large pot.
Fill the pot with water until the jars are covered and
bring the water to a boil. Boil the jars for 45 minutes
and then let them cool in the pot. Store them in a
dark, cool spot.

Duck Confit
(Confit de canard)

RECIPE IS FOR 1 DUCK
PREP TIME: 1 HOUR
COOKING TIME: 2 HOURS
STEEPING TIME: 24 HOURS

1 plump duck, boned

5½ tablespoons salt

1 tablespoon allspice

1 tablespoon black pepper

6 bay leaves, crushed

2 thyme bunches without leaves

Lard

Several sterilized jars (page 253)

1. Divide the duck into quarters so that each piece contains a limb: two pieces with legs and two with wings.

2. Mix the bay leaves, thyme, salt, pepper, and allspice in a small bowl. Then rub each quarter of the duck with the mixture.

3. Put the duck pieces in a large bowl and add the rest of the salt. Then pack the duck pieces down tightly in the bowl and cover the bowl with a plate. Let the duck marinate in the fridge for 24 hours.

4. On the following day, remove the excess salt from the duck pieces. Collect the fat that formed on the surface of the bowl, melt it in a cast-iron pot, and store it in a container. The duck pieces must be covered in fat as they cook, so make sure you have enough on hand.

5. Put the duck quarters and the melted grease in a pan and simmer them gently for two hours. The skin of the duck will turn red. Check the duck by poking one of the pieces with a toothpick; it should go in easily.

6. When the duck quarters have finished cooking, transfer them to the jars. Strain the cooking grease from the pan, pour it into the jars, and let them cool in the fridge. On the following day, pour a little melted lard into each jar—this will insulate the confit.

7. If you plan on storing the confit, seal the jars and place them in a pot. Fill the pot with water so that the jars are completely covered. Boil them for three hours.

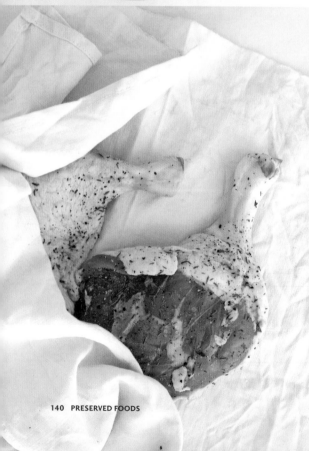

CHAPTER 7

Charcuterie

terrines, cured meat, spreads…

MAKING A TERRINE

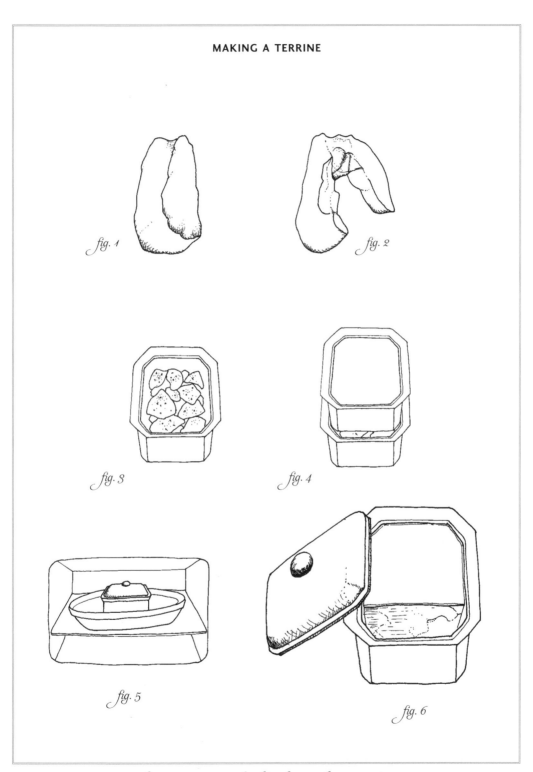

fig. 1: the raw meat ~ fig. 2: breaking the meat down ~ fig. 3: seasoning
fig. 4: applying pressure ~ fig. 5: cooking ~ fig. 6 ~ setting aside

Dry Cured Ham
(Jambon séché)

RECIPE MAKES 1 HAM
PREP TIME: AT LEAST 20 MINUTES
DRYING TIME: 3 TO 4 WEEKS

1 ham

18 ounces canning/pickling salt

6 tablespoons sugar

¾ ounce peppercorns

¾ ounce allspice

⅜ ounce juniper berries

10 cloves

⅜ ounce food-grade saltpeter (potassium nitrate)

Bay leaf, crumbled

Thyme

Pestle or mixer

Curing tub

1. Use a pestle or a mixer to coarsely grind the peppercorns, allspice, juniper berries, and cloves. Then put the mixture in a small bowl and add the bay leaf, salt, potassium nitrate, sugar, and thyme. Mix the ingredients together well.

2. Cut the fat off the rind of the ham with a sharp knife. This should give it a nice round shape. Then remove the hipbone (not the bone you're using to hold the ham, but the one in the middle that's visible on the surface). Beat the rind with a rolling pin to remove any blood. This will also smooth out the rind and make it easier to cut up.

3. Thread a piece of strong rope through the loop of the hock. Then hang the ham up with the rounded part pointing downward in a cool, well-ventilated area. Leave it for three days (five if it's the winter). During this time, the blood will drain out of the ham.

4. Take the ham down and wipe it off thoroughly, taking care to clean the spot where the bone was removed. Put half of the salt mixture from step 1 into the bottom of the curing tub and then place the ham in the tub on its rind. Cover the ham with the rest of the salt mixture. Then put the top on the salting tub and add close to 50 pounds of weight so that the ham is packed down tightly. Leave the ham in the tub for three weeks.

5. Take the ham out of the salting tub, wash it in water, and rinse it. Hang it in a cool, well-ventilated area and let it dry.

6. The ham can be eaten after 15 days, but it's a good idea to wait until the meat has dried thoroughly. If it looks like that might take a while—three or four months—then wrap the ham in a cloth bag so that insects won't bother it and let it hang.

Sausages
(Saucisses)

RECIPE MAKES 4½ POUNDS
PREP TIME: 1 HOUR
SET ASIDE: 1 NIGHT

3½ pounds lean pork shoulder, boned and de-nerved

18 ounces fatty bacon or pork belly

2½ teaspoons super-fine sugar

6½ teaspoons table salt

4 teaspoons black pepper

Small pig intestines

Meat grinder

Kitchen gloves

Food processor
   (or plastic bottle with base cut off, see step 3)

Wooden spoon

String

1. Run the pork shoulder and the fatty pork through the meat grinder. To make Toulouse-style sausages, put the grinder on the coarse setting. To make chipolata-style sausages, use the medium-grind setting. The meat shouldn't be ground finely.

2. Put all of the meat in a large bowl with the salt, sugar, and pepper, and mix well. Wear gloves while mixing. Refrigerate the meat overnight.

3. On the following day, tie off one end of the intestine with string, then fill it with meat using a food processor that has a funnel attachment. You can also use a plastic bottle with the base cut off so that it forms a funnel. If you use the latter, you'll need to pack the meat into the intestine using the handle of a wooden spoon. Pack the meat in consistently to avoid the formation of air pockets. Twist the intestine every 4 inches or so as you work.

Tip
You can pre-cut the intestines to the desired length for your sausages. Shorter pieces are easier to fill. With shorter pieces you also avoid the air bubbles that can form when meat is packed in over the course of several inches.

Dry Cured Sausage

(Saucisson maison)

RECIPE MAKES A DOZEN SAUSAGES
PREP TIME: 1 HOUR
SET ASIDE: 1 NIGHT
DRYING TIME: 2 TO 3 MONTHS

4½ pounds pork shoulder

2¼ pounds fatty bacon

12 feet pork or beef intestine

½ cup red wine

1 clove garlic, crushed

¼ cup table salt

15 black peppercorns

¾ teaspoon super-fine sugar

1 teaspoon ground pepper

1 teaspoon food-grade saltpeter (potassium nitrate)

Meat grinder

String

1. Soak the intestines in cold water while you combine the red wine and the garlic in a bowl. Transfer the intestines to the red wine mixture and steep in the fridge overnight.

2. On the following day, take the intestines out of the wine and let them drain. Strain the wine and set aside.

3. Chop up the other meats using a meat grinder on a coarse setting. You can use a knife to cut up the meats, but make sure they're chopped very finely. Put all of the meat in a large bowl and then add the strained wine, salt, pepper, sugar, and saltpeter. Mix the ingredients thoroughly by hand, with gloves on.

4. Decide on a length for your sausages and cut the intestines to the desired size. Tie off one end of each intestine with butcher's twine.

5. Pack the chopped meat into each intestine. Try to avoid the formation of air pockets as you work

6. Tie off the second end of each intestine with string. Then poke each sausage with a needle to release any air.

7. Hang the sausages in a heated room so that the intestines can dry. After three or four days, move them to a cool, well-ventilated room and hang them up for the extended drying phase. Let them dry for two to three months or longer, depending on your taste.

Notes

• *The sausages will keep for about three months. As with homemade potted meats and pâtés, you must be cautious with sausages. Don't wait too long before eating.*

• *Sausages lose 40% of their weight as they dry. A 14-ounce sausage will weigh only about 9 ounces when it's dry.*

Chicken Liver Pâté
(Pâté de foie)

RECIPE MAKES ABOUT 10 OUNCES
PREP TIME: 15 MINUTES
COOKING TIME: 10 MINUTES
SET ASIDE: 4 HOURS

8 ounces chicken livers, trimmed

²/₃ cup salted butter, softened

1 shallot, finely chopped

2 thyme sprigs

2 bay leaves

2 garlic cloves, finely chopped

2 teaspoons Worcestershire sauce

1 tablespoon cognac

½ teaspoon freshly ground black pepper

1. Melt two tablespoons of butter in a large pan and add the shallot, thyme, bay leaves, and garlic. Cook until the ingredients are tender but not browned.

2. Add the chicken livers, Worcestershire sauce, and cognac, and cook for five minutes. The livers should remain pink in the middle. Set the livers aside for five minutes.

3. Remove the bay leaves and thyme from the mixture. Then add the rest of the butter and the black pepper.

4. Refrigerate for at least four hours.

Note
Store the pâté in a container in the refrigerator. It will keep for five days.

Country Terrine
(Terrine de campagne)

RECIPE SERVES 8 PEOPLE
PREP TIME: 40 MINUTES
STEEPING TIME: 2 HOURS
COOKING TIME: 1½ HOURS
REFRIGERATION TIME: 3 DAYS

9 ounces bacon

9 ounces pork shoulder

9 ounces pork liver

5¼ ounces chicken liver

2½ tablespoons lard

2 onions, peeled

4 garlic cloves, peeled

2 shallots, peeled

2 bay leaves

1 heaping tablespoon flour

7 tablespoons white wine

2 tablespoons salt

1 teaspoon mignonette pepper

½ teaspoon of allspice

1 egg

1. Cut the bacon and pork shoulder into one-inch pieces. Then cut the pork and chicken livers into small cubes.

2. Put the livers and white wine in a bowl. Steep the livers in the wine for an hour at room temperature or in the fridge overnight.

3. Drain the livers and brown them quickly in the lard, just long enough to sear them.

4. Finely mince the garlic, onions, and shallots.

5. Mix the cubes of meat and liver in a large bowl. Then add the mixture from step 4. Add the salt, pepper, allspice, flour, and the egg. Then put on the gloves and knead the ingredients.

6. Pack the mixture into a baking dish and top it with the bay leaves. Cover the baking dish and place it inside a deeper baking dish. Pour cold water into the larger dish and place it in the oven.

7. Bake the terrine for 1½ hours at 350°F.

8. Let the terrine cool after cooking. Refrigerate it for a couple of days before eating.

Liver Terrine
(Terrine de foie gras)

RECIPE SERVES 6 TO 8 PEOPLE
PREP TIME: 1 HOUR
STEEPING TIME: 2 HOURS
COOKING TIME: 20 MINUTES
REFRIGERATION TIME: 3 DAYS

18-21-ounce duck liver or chicken liver

1 tablespoon salt

1 teaspoon black pepper

1 tablespoon sweet red wine, such as Grenache

1. Put the liver on a cutting board and separate the two lobes. Remove the veins with a knife.

2. When the liver is very cold, divide it with your hands. It should split up along the line where the veins used to be. Chop the liver into chunks.

3. Preheat the oven to 450°F. Put the pieces of liver in a baking dish, sprinkle them with salt and pepper, and add the wine.

4. Cover the baking dish and place it inside a deeper baking dish. Pour cold water into the larger dish and place it in the oven.

5. Bake the terrine for 20 minutes.

6. Take the cover off of the baking dish the terrine is in and use a spoon to remove the layer of grease that's floating on the surface. Put the grease in a container and set it aside.

7. Cover the dish with aluminum foil, pressing it down gently. Put a weight (a can of soup will do) on top of the bowl and refrigerate it overnight.

8. On the following day, remove the weight and the foil from the dish. Melt the grease from step 6 and pour it over the terrine. Then cover the terrine again and refrigerate it for at least three days before eating.

Potted Pork
(Rillettes de porc)

RECIPE MAKES 4½ POUNDS
PREP TIME: 45 MINUTES
SET ASIDE: 1 NIGHT
COOKING TIME: 5 HOURS OVER THE COURSE OF 2 DAYS

4½ pounds pork neck (also called pork jowl)

4½ pounds bacon

1½ tablespoons cooking salt

1 teaspoon white pepper

1 teaspoon allspice

3 bay leaves, crushed

1. Remove any cartilage from the pork neck. Cut the pork neck and bacon into small bits.

2. Place the meat in a large cast-iron pot along with half a cup of water. Sprinkle it with salt, pepper, and the bay leaves, and then cover it and let it cook over low heat for three hours. Stir it regularly to keep it from sticking to the bottom of the pot.

3. Set the mixture aside in the fridge for one night.

4. On the following day, put the pot on the stove, uncovered, give it a stir, and add the allspice. Then cook the mixture for two hours over low heat.

5. When the meat has finished cooking, shred it a bit at a time with a knife and fork. Then pack it into jars or bowls, add a little grease for insulation, and put it in the refrigerator.

Note
Potted meat will keep for about two weeks in the refrigerator.

Potted Rabbit
(Rillettes de maquereau)

RECIPE SERVES 6 TO 8 PEOPLE
PREP TIME: 45 MINUTES
COOKING TIME: 4 HOURS
REFRIGERATION TIME: 3 DAYS

1 large rabbit cut into pieces

12 ounces fatty pork loin

7 ounces bacon or pork belly

1¾ ounces lard

2 onions

2 bay leaves

Allspice

Salt

Black pepper

1 small chili pepper, dried (optional)

1. Cut the pork loin and bacon into large cubes. Melt the lard in a large pot and add the pork, the rabbit, and about two cups of water.

2. Add a couple of pinches of salt and pepper (or the chili pepper), the bay leaf, and allspice. Cook the ingredients for four hours over low heat, checking regularly to make sure that nothing sticks to the bottom of the pot. If something does start to stick, add a splash of lukewarm water to the mixture.

3. When the rabbit can be shredded with a fork, take it off the heat and shred the meat.

4. Put the shredded meat in a large mixing bowl, add most of the remaining fat from the cooked meats, and mix well.

5. Transfer the mixture to a baking dish or bowl and cover it with a little additional grease to preserve the meat. Refrigerate for three days before eating.

Note

Don't be put off by all of the fatty pieces listed in the ingredients. Rabbit meat is very lean and dry, and only becomes tender when cooked with fatty meats. If you make the recipe once and decide you could make do with less fat, just cut down on the amount used the next time you make the recipe or add less fat back into the rabbit in step 4.

Potted Mackerel
(Rillettes de maquereau)

RECIPE SERVES 6 TO 8 PEOPLE
PREP TIME: 30 MINUTES
COOKING TIME: 20 MINUTES
REFRIGERATION TIME: 4 HOURS

3⅓ pounds mackerel filets

1 onion, peeled and sliced

1 carrot, peeled and sliced

1 bunch flat-leaved parsley, finely chopped

Bay leaf

Thyme

1 teaspoon coriander seeds

3 cups dry white wine

4 tablespoons Meaux mustard

6 tablespoons olive oil

2 tablespoons cider vinegar

Salt

Black pepper

1. Place the carrot, onion, white wine, thyme, bay leaf, and coriander into a large pan. Add pepper and one handful of cooking salt. Bring the mixture to a boil. Turn off the heat and let the sauce cool down.

2. Wipe the filets thoroughly with a paper towel. Then place them in the sauce and let them simmer for 10 minutes.

3. When the filets have cooled, take them out of the sauce. Remove the skin and bones and shred them with a fork.

4. Mix the mustard and vinegar in a bowl, gradually adding the olive oil as you stir. The mixture should thicken to a consistency like mayonnaise.

5. Add the shredded mackerel and the parsley to the mustard mixture and stir. Store the mackerel in a covered container in the refrigerator before serving.

Smoked Salmon
(Saumon fumé maison)

RECIPE SERVES 4 PEOPLE
PREP TIME: 5 MINUTES
COOKING TIME: 10 MINUTES

4 salmon filets with skin on, about 4½ ounces each
2 tablespoons smoked tea (such as Lapsang Souchong)
Oil
Salt

1. Place the tea on the bottom of the pot or wok. Then lightly oil the rack.

2. Salt the salmon filets and place them on the rack (the skin side of the fish should be touching the rack). Cover the wok or pot loosely so that smoke will be able to escape.

3. Put the pot on the stove over very low heat. Let the salmon smoke for five to 10 minutes.

4. Close the lid and let the fish cool inside the container for an hour or so. Once it's cool, wrap it in plastic and put it in the fridge.

Note
Wrapped in plastic and refrigerated, the salmon will keep for about a week. If you decide to freeze the fish, it'll be good for six months.

Tarama with Salmon Roe
(Tarama aux oeufs de saumon)

RECIPE SERVES 4 PEOPLE
PREP TIME: 15 MINUTES

7 ounces faissalle (page 46), thoroughly drained

2½ ounces salmon roe

1¾ ounces sandwich bread with crusts removed

1 tablespoon olive oil

1 tablespoon lemon juice

Salt

Pepper

1. Put half of the salmon roe and half of the faissalle in a blender with the sandwich bread, olive oil, and lemon juice. Blend until smooth.

2. Add the rest of the faissalle and salmon roe. Then stir the ingredients gently. They should be mixed well but not whipped in texture. Add salt and pepper to taste.

3. Transfer the tarama to a bowl and store it in the refrigerator for a few hours before serving.

Hummus with Roasted Bell Pepper
(Houmous au poivron grille)

RECIPE MAKES 14 OUNCES
PREP TIME: 15 MINUTES
COOKING TIME (FOR THE PEPPERS): 40 MINUTES

3 large red bell peppers, coarsely chopped

4½ ounces canned chickpeas, rinsed and drained

Olive oil

½ garlic clove, peeled and crushed

1 teaspoon freshly squeezed lemon juice

1 teaspoon of tahini

1 teaspoon ground cumin

1 pinch of sugar

Salt

Pepper

1. Preheat your oven to 400°F.

2. Arrange the peppers on a baking sheet and sprinkle them with olive oil. Bake them in the oven for 40 minutes, then take them out and let them cool to room temperature.

3. Blend all of the ingredients with a food processor or blender until they form a coarse paste. Add salt and pepper as desired. Transfer the hummus to a container and refrigerate.

Variation

You can make Traditional Hummus (Houmous classique) by omitting the bell pepper, using 7 ounces of chickpeas, 2 to 4 tablespoons of extra-virgin olive oil, and the rest of the ingredients at left.

Tapenade
(Tapenade)

RECIPE SERVES SIX TO EIGHT PEOPLE
PREP TIME: 20 MINUTES

9 ounces black olives, pitted

3½ tablespoons capers

10 anchovy filets in salt, rinsed and drained

10 tablespoons olive oil

Juice of ½ lemon

Black pepper

Combine the black olives, capers, anchovies, lemon juice, and black pepper in a blender. Purée the ingredients as you add the olive oil.

Note

The sauce will keep for two months in the refrigerator. Just pour it into a jar, add a thin layer of olive oil, and seal.

Green Tapenade
(Tapenade verte)

RECIPE SERVES SIX TO EIGHT PEOPLE
PREP TIME: 20 MINUTES

9 ounces green olives, pitted

3½ tablespoons blanched almonds

2 tablespoons capers

6 anchovy filets, rinsed and drained

8 tablespoons olive oil

Black pepper

Put the green olives, almonds, capers, anchovy filets, and a bit of pepper in a blender. Purée the ingredients as you add the olive oil.

Tapeno

Tapenade comes from the Provençal word *tapeno*, which means *caper*. You can easily make delicious variations on the traditional tapenade—just be sure the recipes contain capers! To create an irresistible red tapenade, try replacing the olives with sun-dried tomatoes or tomatoes marinated in garlic and oil.

Eggplant Dip
(Caviar d'aubergines)

RECIPE MAKES 18 OUNCES
PREP TIME: 15 MINUTES
COOKING TIME: 1 HOUR

3 eggplants without stems

4 garlic cloves, peeled

1 bunch basil

Cumin seeds

½ teaspoon paprika

4 tablespoons olive oil

Salt

Black pepper

1. Bake the eggplants in the oven at 350°F, turning them regularly until they blacken and become soft to the touch. Depending on the oven, this should take 45 minutes to an hour.

2. Remove the eggplants from the oven, cut them in half, and scoop out their flesh with a spoon. Put the flesh in a mixer or blender along with the cumin seeds, garlic, paprika, salt, and pepper. Add a trickle of olive oil while the mixer is turning and mix or blend until you have a smooth consistency.

3. Transfer the dip to a covered container and store it in the refrigerator before serving.

Anchoïade
(Anchoïade)

RECIPE SERVES FOUR TO SIX PEOPLE
PREP TIME: 30 MINUTES

10 anchovy filets in salt or 20 filets in oil

3 cloves garlic, peeled and crushed

½ bunch flat-leaf parsley

8 tablespoons olive oil

Juice of ½ lemon

Black pepper

Electric mixer

1. If the anchovies are in oil, drain them. If they're in salt, rinse them in lukewarm water. Then prepare them: Take one of the anchovies and place it on your work surface. To remove the skin, hold it by the tail as you scrape along its length (on both sides) with the knife. If the anchovy has a fin, pull it off along with any bones that might be attached. Then scrape the spine so that the anchovy opens up and lies flat, grasp the spine at the tail end and pull it out. You should now have two boneless fillets. Use a knife to remove any intestines. Repeat with the rest of the anchovies and rinse them again in cool water.

2. Place the anchovies in water and let them soak for 15 minutes.

3. Wash the parsley and then cut the stalks just over an inch away from the leaves.

4. Put the anchovy filets, lemon juice, garlic, parsley, olive oil, and pepper into the mixer and blend until smooth.

Note

If you plan to use the anchoïade as a spread, mix it until it has a somewhat coarse consistency. If you plan to use it as a dip with raw vegetables, mix it longer or use a blender.

Sweet Potato Chips
(Chips de patate douce)

RECIPE SERVES 4 PEOPLE
PREP TIME: 20 MINUTES
COOKING TIME: 5 MINUTES

3 sweet potatoes
Oil for frying, such as canola or peanut
Salt

1. Peel the sweet potatoes and cut them into very thin slices (use a mandoline slicer, if possible).

2. Heat a few inches of oil in a deep pan to 350°F. Put the sweet potato slices in the hot oil and let them brown. They should brown quickly, in three to four minutes.

3. Transfer the chips to a pan lined with paper towels and let them drain. Add salt as desired.

Variation

You can also make Parsnip Chips (chips de panais) or Beet Chips (chips de betterave). Follow the same steps as above, but substitute 3 parsnips or 4 beets in place of the sweet potatoes.

CHAPTER 8

Sweet spreads
jellies, jams, compotes...

JAM-MAKING MATERIALS

fig. 1

fig. 2

fig. 3

fig. 4

fig. 6

fig. 7

fig. 5

fig. 8

fig. 1-5 : fruits ~ fig. 6 : jam pan ~ fig. 7 : skimming ladle ~ fig. 8 : jars

Strawberry Jam
(Confiture de fraises)

RECIPE FILLS SIX 8-OUNCE JARS
PREP TIME: 10 MINUTES
SET ASIDE: 1 NIGHT
COOKING TIME: 20 MINUTES

2¼ pounds strawberries

4½ cups granulated sugar

Juice of 1 lemon

6 sterilized jars (page 253)

1. Wash the strawberries in cool water, dry them with a dish towel, and remove their stems with a small knife. Then put them in a bowl with the sugar and lemon juice. Cover the bowl and refrigerate the berries overnight.

2. Crush the berries in a colander and pour the collected juice into a large, thick-bottomed pan. Heat the juice, stirring it with a wooden spoon until it comes to a boil, and add the strawberries. Boil the mixture for about five minutes. Then drain the strawberries over a bowl.

3. Cook the collected juice over medium heat for five minutes, then put the strawberries back in and bring the mixture to a boil. Boil the jam for six minutes, carefully stirring it with a wooden spoon. Use a skimming ladle to remove the foam that forms on the surface.

4. Using a small ladle, transfer the jam to the jars while still hot, cap them, and turn them upside down. Let the jam cool and then store it in a dark, dry spot.

Note

Turning the jars upside down after capping them is an important precaution, as it prevents the formation of mold on the surface of the jam and provides a more secure seal.

Raspberry Jam
(Confiture de framboises)

RECIPE FILLS SIX 8-OUNCE JARS
PREP TIME: 10 MINUTES
COOKING TIME: 12 MINUTES

1¼ pounds raspberries

4 cups granulated sugar

Juice of 1 lemon

6 sterilized jars (page 253)

1. Rinse the raspberries in cool water and let them drain. Then put the raspberries, sugar, and lemon juice into a large, thick-bottomed pan.

2. Bring the ingredients in the pan to a boil over medium-high heat while stirring them with a wooden spoon. Simmer for about 10 minutes. Use a skimming ladle to remove the foam that forms on the surface.

3. Using a small ladle, transfer the jam to the jars, cap them, and turn them upside down. Let the jars cool and then store them in a dark, dry spot.

Note

Turning the jars upside down after capping them is an important precaution, as it prevents the formation of mold on the surface of the jam and provides a more secure seal.

Redcurrant Jelly
(Gelée de groseille)

RECIPE FILLS FOUR 8-OUNCE JARS
PREP TIME: 15 MINUTES
COOKING TIME: 15 MINUTES

8 cups redcurrants

5½ cups granulated sugar

Juice of 1 lemon

Large square of muslin

4 sterilized jars (page 253)

1. Rinse the redcurrants in cool water, let them drain, and place them on the muslin. Gather the corners of the muslin together and tie them with string to form a sack with the fruit inside. Then squeeze the sack tightly over a large bowl. The bowl will catch the redcurrant juice that's produced by squeezing.

2. Transfer the juice to a jam pan or thick-bottomed pan, and add the sugar and lemon juice. Cook the ingredients over medium heat for about 15 minutes.

3. Using a small ladle, transfer the jelly to the jars. Let the jars cool and then store them in a dark, dry spot.

Note
Turning the jars upside down after capping them is an important precaution, as it prevents the formation of mold on the surface of the jam and provides a more secure seal.

Orange Marmalade
(Marmelade d'oranges)

RECIPE FILLS SEVEN 8-OUNCE JARS
PREP TIME: 25 MINUTES
COOKING TIME: 1 HOUR

15 oranges (Seville is traditional but you can use Valencia for a sweeter marmelade)

2¼ pounds granulated sugar

Juice of 1 lemon

7 sterilized jars (page 253)

1. Rinse the oranges under cool water and wipe them dry. Using a vegetable peeler, remove the skin from three of the oranges. Cut the peels into strips about an inch in length.

2. Put the peel slices in a pan filled with water and bring them to a slow boil. Cook them until they're tender and drain.

3. Squeeze all of the oranges into a large, thick-bottomed pan, and add the sugar and lemon juice. Cook the mixture over medium heat for 50 minutes, stirring continually with a wooden spoon. Add the peel slices from step 2 and continue cooking for 20 minutes. Use a skimmer to remove the foam that forms on the surface.

4. Using a small ladle, transfer the marmalade to the jars, cap them, and turn them upside down. Let the jars cool and then store them in a dark, dry spot.

Note

Turning the jars upside down after capping them is an important precaution, as it prevents the formation of mold on the surface of the jam and provides a more secure seal.

Plum Jam
(Confiture de quetsches)

RECIPE FILLS FOUR 9-OUNCE JARS
PREP TIME: 10 MINUTES
SET ASIDE: 1 NIGHT
COOKING TIME: 20 MINUTES

2¼ pounds plums (use damson plums if you can find them)

4½ cups granulated sugar

Juice of 1 lemon

4 sterilized jars (page 253)

1. Rinse the plums in cool water, let them drain, and dry them with a dish towel. Then cut them in half and remove the stones.

2. Combine the plums, sugar, and lemon juice in a large bowl. Cover the bowl and refrigerate it overnight.

3. On the following day, transfer the contents of the bowl to a large, thick-bottomed pan. Bring the ingredients to a boil over high heat while stirring them with a wooden spoon. Use a skimmer to remove the foam that forms on the surface of the pan.

4. Using a small ladle, transfer the jam to the jars, cap them, and turn them upside down. Let the jars cool and then store them in a dark, cool spot.

Apricot Jam
(Confiture d'abricots)

RECIPE MAKES FOUR 9-OUNCE JARS
PREP TIME: 15 MINUTES
SET ASIDE: 1 NIGHT
COOKING TIME: 20 MINUTES

1⅓ pounds ripe, firm apricots

2 cups granulated sugar

Juice of ½ lemon

4 sterilized jars (page 253)

1. Rinse the apricots in cool water, let them drain, and dry them with a clean dish towel. Cut them in two and remove the stones.

2. Combine the apricot pieces, sugar, and lemon juice in a large bowl. Cover the bowl and refrigerate it overnight.

3. On the following day, transfer the contents of the bowl to a large, thick-bottomed pan. Bring the mixture to a boil over high heat while stirring it with a wooden spoon. Then cook the mixture over medium heat for 20 minutes, stirring it continually. Use a skimmer to remove the foam that forms on the surface.

4. Using a small ladle, transfer the jam to the jars, cap them, and turn them upside down. Let the jars cool and then store them in a dark, cool spot.

Apple-Vanilla Compote

(Compote pomme-vanille)

RECIPE SERVES 4 PEOPLE
PREP TIME: 10 MINUTES
COOKING TIME: 10 MINUTES

4 large apples, peeled, cored, and cut into pieces

1 vanilla pod

¼ cup water

1 tablespoon lemon juice

1. Using a cutting board and knife, cut the vanilla pod in half lengthwise. Scrape each half of the pod with the dull side of your knife to remove the seeds. Then put the seeds in a pan with the pod halves, water, lemon juice, and apples. Cook the ingredients for 10 minutes over high heat, stirring continuously. If the preparation seems dry, add a little water.

2. When the apples have softened (but before they turn too mushy), remove them from the heat and crush them into chunks with a fork. Remove the vanilla pod from the mixture at this time.

3. Let the compote cool and store it in the fridge. Eat it within two or three days.

Note

This compote will keep just fine in the freezer.

Apple-Banana Compote

(Compote pomme-banane)

RECIPE SERVES 4 PEOPLE
PREP TIME: 10 MINUTES
COOKING TIME: 10 MINUTES

4 large apples

1 banana

¼ cup water

1 tablespoon lemon juice

1. Peel the apples, core them, and cut them into small pieces. Peel and slice the banana.

2. Put the fruit in a pan with the water and lemon juice and bring the ingredients to a boil. Cook for 10 minutes over high heat, stirring continuously. If the mixture seems dry, add a little water.

3. When the apples start to come apart, remove the mixture from the heat. The banana will melt completely during the cooking. This compote is best enjoyed when it's still slightly warm.

Strawberry-Rhubarb Compote

(Compote rhubarbe-fraise)

RECIPE SERVES 4 TO 6 PEOPLE
PREP TIME: 10 MINUTES
COOKING TIME: 15 TO 20 MINUTES

2¼ pounds rhubarb

7 ounces strawberries

9 ounces brown sugar

1 teaspoon lemon juice

1 tablespoon water

1. Wash the rhubarb stalks, skin them with a paring knife, and cut them into small slices.

2. Rinse the strawberries, remove the stems with a small knife, and cut them in half.

3. In a large pan, cook the rhubarb, sugar, lemon juice, and water for 10 minutes over high heat, stirring regularly. When the rhubarb begins to break down, add the strawberries. Continue cooking for five to 10 minutes. Let the mixture cool and then stir it until the ingredients are well blended.

4. The compote should be eaten the day you make it. Serve it cool.

Pear-Raspberry Compote
(Compote poire-framboise)

RECIPE SERVES 3 TO 4 PEOPLE
PREP TIME: 10 MINUTES
COOKING TIME: 10 MINUTES

3 ripe pears

11 ounces raspberries

6½ tablespoons cane sugar

3 pinches agar-agar powder

1 tablespoon water

1 tablespoon poppy seeds (optional)

4 mint leaves (optional)

1. Peel the pears, core them, and cut them into quarters. Rinse the raspberries in water and let them drain.

2. Combine the pear quarters, raspberries, sugar, agar-agar, and water in a large pan and bring them to a boil. Cook the ingredients over high heat for seven to eight minutes, stirring regularly.

3. The compote will thicken as it cools. Add poppy seeds and mint leaves before serving, if desired.

Tip
The agar-agar serves as a thickener in this recipe. Without it, the compote will be runnier but just as delicious.

Chocolate-Hazelnut Spread
(Pâte à tartiner choco-noisette)

RECIPE MAKES 10 OUNCES
PREP TIME: 10 MINUTES
COOKING TIME: 10 MINUTES

5 ounces skinless whole hazelnuts

5 ounces dark chocolate

2 tablespoons sunflower oil

2 tablespoons confectioners sugar

½ teaspoon pure vanilla extract

Salt

Blender

Sterilized jar (page 253)

1. Preheat the oven to 350°F. Spread the hazelnuts out on a baking sheet and roast them in the oven for 10 minutes. Let them cool.

2. Melt the chocolate in a double boiler. Stir it occasionally so that it becomes smooth. Let it cool to room temperature.

3. Using a blender, blend the hazelnuts into a fine powder and then add the oil, sugar, vanilla, and salt. Blend the ingredients into a paste, and then add the chocolate. Blend again until the ingredients are combined.

4. Transfer the spread to a sterilized jar and store it in a cool, dark spot.

Note
The spread will keep for two weeks unopened. Store it in the fridge after opening.

Variation
Replace the hazelnuts in this recipe with the nuts of your choice—almonds, macadamia nuts, peanuts, pistachios, or cashews.

White Chocolate Spread
(Pâte à tartinerau chocolat blanc)

RECIPE MAKES 14 OUNCES
PREP TIME: 5 MINUTES
COOKING TIME: 15 MINUTES
REFRIGERATION TIME: 15 MINUTES

9 ounces white chocolate cut into small pieces

10 tablespoons whole liquid cream

Salt

Sterilized jar (page 253)

1. Melt the chocolate in a double boiler. Stir it occasionally until it becomes smooth. Let it cool to room temperature.

2. Add the cream and salt to the chocolate and stir. If any lumps appear, put the double boiler back on the heat and stir until the lumps disappear.

3. Let the spread set for 15 minutes in the refrigerator. Stored in the fridge, it will last for two weeks.

Serving the spread
If the spread hardens before serving, heat it gently in a double boiler or microwave it for about 30 seconds.

Chestnut Cream
(Crème de marrons)

RECIPE MAKES 10 OUNCES
PREP TIME: 5 MINUTES
COOKING TIME: 15 MINUTES

7 ounces chestnuts (frozen or from a jar)

1 vanilla bean, cut in half

10 tablespoons heavy cream

2½ tablespoons brown sugar

1½ tablespoons cognac

Blender

Container with lid

1. Scrape the vanilla pod to remove the seeds. Put the seeds and the pod in a pan with the chestnuts, cream, brown sugar, and cognac. Simmer the ingredients over low heat for 15 minutes, stirring occasionally.

2. Let the mixture cool and remove the vanilla pod. Using the blender, blend the ingredients until they form a paste. If the paste seems too thick, add a little more heavy cream. Store in a sealed container.

Note

The chestnut cream should be refrigerated. It will keep for about two weeks.

Salted Caramel Spread
(Caramel au beurre salé)

RECIPE MAKES 12 OUNCES
PREP TIME: 5 MINUTES
COOKING TIME: 10 MINUTES
REFRIGERATION TIME: 10 TO 15 MINUTES

1¼ cup sugar

6¾ tablespoons water

⅔ cup soft butter

½ cup heavy cream

1 teaspoon sea salt

Container with lid

1. In a large pan, gently heat the sugar and the water, stirring occasionally until the ingredients have browned. Then add the liquid cream and sea salt.

2. Bring the mixture to a boil and cook it at a rolling boil for five minutes, stirring occasionally. The mixture should take on the consistency of caramel, becoming thick and turning a dark golden brown. Watch the mixture carefully once it starts to take on color—it happens fast, and the mixture can easily burn.

3. When the mixture has a nice caramel color, remove it immediately from the heat. Stir it until it cools down and is warm to the touch. Then refrigerate it for 10 to 15 minutes.

4. Beat the butter in a small bowl until it's creamy then stir it into the cooled caramel. Transfer the caramel to your storage container and seal the lid tightly. It will keep for about two weeks in the fridge.

Tip
If the caramel is too hard when you're ready to serve it, microwave it for about 30 seconds.

Lemon Curd
(Lemon curd)

RECIPE MAKES 16 OUNCES
PREP TIME: 15 MINUTES
COOKING TIME: 20 MINUTES

½ cup fresh-squeezed lemon juice

1 cup sugar

3 eggs

⅔ cup soft butter cut into small cubes

1 pinch salt

Container with lid

1. Using a whisk, mix the juice, sugar, eggs, and salt in a medium-sized pan. Add the butter and then cook the mixture over low heat, whisking continuously until the butter is melted.

2. Turn up the heat and cook the mixture while whisking it. When it thickens and begins to take on the consistency of jelly, remove it from the heat. The curd is ready when it coats the back of a spoon.

3. Immediately strain the curd and pour it into a container with a tight-fitting lid. The curd will keep for about three weeks in the refrigerator.

Variation

Replace the lemon juice with the juice of four limes, a medium grapefruit, or two oranges.

CHAPTER 9

Sweet treats

cookies, granola, ice cream...

CANDYING FRUIT

fig. 1

fig. 2

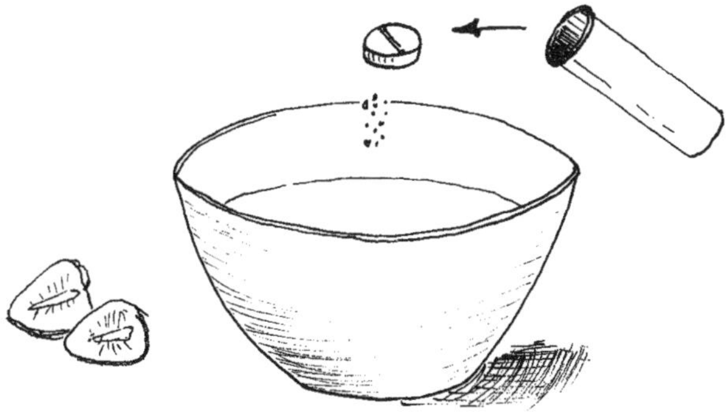

fig. 3

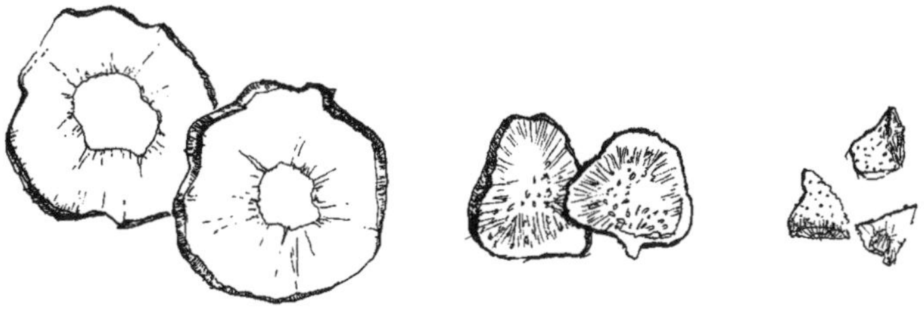

fig. 1 : fruits - fig. 2 : placing the fruits into water with sugar - fig. 3 : drying out the fruit

Cat's Tongue Cookies
(Langues-de-chat)

RECIPE MAKES 30 COOKIES
PREP TIME: 20 MINUTES
COOKING TIME: 6 MINUTES

½ cup flour

3½ tablespoons cooled, salted butter cut into cubes +
   1½ tablespoons for cookie sheet

8 tablespoons confectioner's sugar

1 egg white

1. Preheat the oven to 350°F.

2. Mix the confectioner's sugar and butter until the mixture is smooth and creamy.

3. Beat the egg white until it forms stiff peaks and stir it into the butter and sugar mixture. Then add the flour, sprinkling it in little by little as you stir.

4. Scoop the dough into a pastry bag with a ¼-inch icing tube. Then squeeze the dough out onto a lightly buttered baking sheet in thin, 1½-inch lengths. The cookies will expand as they bake, so space them about an inch apart on the sheet.

5. Bake the cookies for six minutes. Check them regularly. They should bake to a golden color and turn slightly brown around the edges. Let the cookies cool and enjoy!

French Butter Cookies
(Palets bretons)

RECIPE MAKES 40 COOKIES
PREP TIME: 15 MINUTES
COOKING TIME: 15 MINUTES

2 cups flour

1½ cups super-fine sugar

1¼ cup salted butter, cut into small cubes +
   1 tablespoon salted butter for the molds

5 egg yolks + 1 egg yolk for brushing

½ packet baking powder

Small round muffin tins or cookie molds

1. Preheat the oven to 350°F.

2. Mix the flour and baking powder together in a bowl. Form the mixture into a pile, create a hollow in the center, and add the 5 egg yolks, sugar, and salt. Combine the ingredients thoroughly with your hands until the mixture has a sandy consistency. Add the cubes of butter, and mix with a spoon.

3. Lightly butter each of the molds and fill them with the dough. Using a brush, baste the top of each piece of dough with a little beaten egg yolk.

4. Put the cookies in the oven for about 15 minutes (the baking time will depend on the thickness of the cookies). Turn the cookies out of the tins or molds while they're still warm and let them cool on a pastry rack.

Almond Tuiles

(Tuiles aux amandes)

RECIPE MAKES 30 COOKIES
PREP TIME: 20 MINUTES
BAKING TIME: 8 MINUTES

2 egg whites

½ cup confectioner's sugar

2 tablespoons salted butter, melted + 1½ tablespoons for baking sheet

¼ cup flour

½ cup chopped or slivered almonds

1. Preheat the oven to 400°F.

2. Whip the egg whites and the confectioner's sugar until they're slightly frothy. Then stir in the flour and melted butter. Mix with a spatula.

3. Butter a baking sheet and dust it lightly with flour. Arrange small piles of the dough on the sheet about an inch apart. Smooth out the piles with the blade of a knife, sprinkle them with almonds, and bake them in the oven for about eight minutes.

4. Take the cookies out of the oven. While they're warm, lift them off the baking sheet with a spatula and drape them over a rolling pin or clean bottle so that they take on an arched shape. Make sure the cookies don't touch. Let them cool for about a minute before removing them. The cookies will be fragile, so handle them with care!

Spice Bread
(Pain d'épice)

RECIPE SERVES 6 PEOPLE
PREP TIME: 15 MINUTES
BAKING TIME: 50 MINUTES

¾ cup honey

2 cups whole-wheat bread flour or 50-50 mixture
    whole-wheat bread flour and rye flour

1¾ ounces almond meal

6¾ tablespoons milk

1 egg

2 teaspoons baking powder

1 tablespoon pumpkin pie spice mix

1½ ounce orange peel, minced

1½ tablespoons butter

Bread pan

1. Preheat the oven to 350°F.

2. Combine the milk and honey in a saucepan and heat them gradually. Remove the mixture from the heat as soon as it starts to bubble.

3. Mix the flour and baking powder in a bowl. Add the almond powder, spices, and orange peel and mix well

4. Create a hole in the middle of the mixture. Pour in the milk and honey preparation from step 2, continually stirring the ingredients with a spoon. Add the egg and stir thoroughly.

5. Butter the bread pan, add the dough, and bake it in the oven for about 50 minutes.

6. Remove the bread from the oven and let it cool on a rack before cutting.

Homemade spice-bread mixture

Instead of pumpkin pie spice mix, try a mix of your own to make the bread. A blend of cinnamon, clove, ginger, and anise is very tasty.

Traditional Muesli
(Muesli classique)

RECIPE SERVES 1 PERSON
PREP TIME: 5 MINUTES
COOKING TIME: 3 MINUTES

6 tablespoons oats

2 tablespoons dried fruits, chopped

1 tablespoon nuts, chopped

1 tablespoon mixed seeds (sunflower, sesame, poppy, flax)

1 teaspoon powdered milk

1 teaspoon brown sugar

1. Toast the nuts, oats, and seeds together in a frying pan (without oil) for two to three minutes. Let them cool.

2. Transfer the mixture to a bowl and combine with the fruit, powdered milk, and brown sugar. Serve with milk or yogurt.

All-Chocolate Muesli
(Muesli tout choco)

RECIPE SERVES 1 PERSON
PREP TIME: 5 MINUTES
COOKING TIME: 3 MINUTES

6 tablespoons oats

2 tablespoons chocolate cereal

2 tablespoons chocolate, chopped

1 teaspoon powdered cocoa

1 tablespoon cocoa beans, slivered

1 teaspoon brown sugar

1. Roast the oats in a frying pan (without oil) for two to three minutes. Let them cool.

2. Transfer the oats to a bowl and combine with the cereal, chopped chocolate, powdered cocoa, cocoa beans, and brown sugar. Serve with milk or yogurt.

Winter Muesli
(Muesli pour l'hiver)

RECIPE SERVES 1 PERSON
PREP TIME: 5 MINUTES
COOKING TIME: 3 MINUTES

6 tablespoons oats

3 tablespoons dried apples, chopped

2 tablespoons nuts, chopped

2 tablespoons mixed seeds (sunflower, sesame, poppy, flax)

1 teaspoon powdered milk

1 teaspoon brown sugar

½ tablespoon ground cinnamon

Ginger

1. Roast the oats in a frying pan (without oil) for two to three minutes. Let them cool.

2. Transfer the oats to a bowl and combine with the apple, nuts, seeds, milk, brown sugar, cinnamon, and a pinch of ginger. Serve with milk or yogurt.

No-Bake Cereal Bars

(Barres de céréales sans cuisson)

RECIPE MAKES 5 TO 6 BARS
PREP TIME: 14 MINUTES
SET ASIDE: 4 HOURS MINIMUM

5 ounces date paste

3½ ounces dried apricots

2 ounces dried figs

7 ounces mixed nuts (hazelnuts, almonds, walnuts, pecans)

½ cup oats or almond meal

1 pinch salt

1 pinch of ground cinnamon

1 pinch ground ginger

Vegetable oil

1. Put all of the ingredients except the vegetable oil into a food processor and mix them until the nuts are chopped into small pieces. Make sure the nuts and the date paste are thoroughly mixed. You can also mix the ingredients by hand as long as you crush the nuts and chop the apricots and figs first.

2. Grease the bottom and sides of a small rectangular pan with the vegetable oil. Add the mixture from step 1, packing it down with the back of a spoon so that it's smooth and even in the pan. Let it set in the refrigerator for a few hours or overnight.

3. Cut the dough into bars with a knife or use a cookie cutter to cut them into the desired shape. If you store the bars in a sealed container, they'll be good for a week.

Traditional Cereal Bars

(Barres de céréales classiques)

RECIPE MAKES 12 BARS
PREP TIME: 10 MINUTES
COOKING TIME: 15 TO 25 MINUTES

1¾ cups oats

3½ ounces dried fruit, chopped

1¾ ounces nuts (hazelnuts, almonds, walnuts, pecans), chopped

4 tablespoons mixed seeds

8 tablespoons sunflower seeds

2 tablespoons brown sugar

⅓ cup agave syrup, maple syrup, or golden syrup

⅓ cup vegetable oil

1. Preheat the oven to 350°F.

2. Melt the sugar, syrup, and oil in a pan over medium heat.

3. Mix all of the dry ingredients together in a bowl and then stir in the syrup mixture from step 2.

4. Line a rectangular pan with wax paper and spread the mixture over it with a large spoon or knife, thoroughly covering the whole surface.

5. Bake for 15 to 20 minutes if you want soft bars. Bake for 25 minutes if you want them to be a bit crunchier.

6. Remove the pan from the oven and let it cool for 10 minutes. While the cereal is still warm, cut it into rectangles.

Gluten-free Chocolate Granola

(Granola sans gluten aux 3 chocolats)

RECIPE MAKES ABOUT 2¼ POUNDS
PREP TIME: 10 MINUTES
COOKING TIME: 45 MINUTES

3½ ounces dark chocolate, coarsely chopped

3½ ounces milk chocolate, coarsely chopped

3½ ounces white chocolate, coarsely chopped

1¾ cups buckwheat flakes

⅔ cup millet

¾ cup buckwheat flakes

¾ ounce puffed rice

¾ ounce puffed quinoa

1½ ounces cocoa nibs

1 cup agave nectar, maple syrup, or honey

2 tablespoons sunflower oil

½ cup cocoa powder

1 teaspoon salt

1. Preheat the oven to 320°F.

2. Heat the agave nectar, maple syrup, or honey, sunflower oil, and cocoa powder in a pan until the mixture is warm and less syrupy. It should stir easily.

3. In a large bowl, mix all of the dry ingredients together except for the three chocolates. Then add the syrup mixture from step 2. Stir the ingredients together thoroughly.

4. Using a knife or large spoon, spread the mixture on two baking sheets. Bake for about 45 minutes, stirring every 10 minutes, until the granola is evenly browned.

5. Remove the granola from the oven and let it cool. Then stir in the three chopped chocolates. Serve with milk or yogurt.

Traditional Granola

(Granola classique)

RECIPE MAKES 2¼ POUNDS
PREP TIME: 10 MINUTES
COOKING TIME: 45 MINUTES

2 cups mixture of buckwheat and large oat flakes

3½ ounces mixed seeds (squash, sunflower, sesame, flax, poppy)

3½ ounces mixed nuts, chopped

7 ounces dried fruit, chopped

7 ounces apple or other fruit compote (blend compote if it has too many pieces)

⅔ cup agave nectar or maple syrup

2 tablespoons sunflower oil

2 teaspoons ground cinnamon

1 teaspoon salt

1. Preheat the oven to 325°F.

2. Heat the syrup, the sunflower oil, and the fruit compote in a pan until the mixture becomes less syrupy and easy to stir.

3. In a large bowl, mix all of the dry ingredients together except for the dried fruit. Then add the syrup mixture from step 2. Stir the ingredients together thoroughly.

4. Using a large knife or spoon, spread the mixture on two baking sheets. Bake for about 45 minutes, stirring every 10 minutes, until the granola is evenly browned.

Pears in Natural Syrup
(*Poires au naturel*)

RECIPE MAKES 1 QUART
PREP TIME: 15 MINUTES
COOKING TIME: 15 MINUTES

2¾ pounds ripe but still firm pears
2 tablespoons super-fine sugar
Juice of 1 lemon
Sterilized jar (page 253)

1. Wash the pears in cool water, dry them, and peel them. You can leave them whole or cut them into quarters. If you cut them up, make sure you remove the stems and the seeds.

2. Put the pears in the jar, sprinkle them with sugar, and add the lemon juice. Seal the jar tightly and put it in a large pot filled with water. Boil the jar for about 15 minutes and then let it cool down in the pan. Store it in a dark, cool spot.

Tip
Add a vanilla pod or small stick of cinnamon for some extra flavor.

Clementines in Syrup

(Clémentines au sirop)

RECIPE MAKES TWO 18-OUNCE JARS
PREP TIME: 15 MINUTES
COOKING TIME: 1 HOUR

1¼ pounds untreated clementines

2½ cups super-fine sugar

1 quart water

2 sterilized jars (page 253)

1. Wash and dry the clementines. Put them in a pot of cold water, bring the water to a boil, and then turn down the heat. Simmer the clementines for about 12 minutes and then drain them.

2. Combine the sugar and water in a thick-bottomed pan, heat slowly, and then add the clementines. Let the fruit simmer for about 30 minutes and then drain it.

3. Transfer the clementines to the jars along with the syrup. Seal the jars tightly and put them in a large pot filled with water. Boil the jars for about 15 minutes and then let them cool down in the pan. Store them in a dark, cool spot.

Preserves in syrup

Using a syrup made with water and sugar to preserve your fruit will ensure that it retains its flavor and color. To make an extra-tasty syrup, add cinnamon or vanilla to the recipe above. Or try spiking the syrup with a spirit like rum or brandy.

Cherries in Brandy
(Cerises à l'eau-de-vie)

RECIPE FILLS ONE 50-OUNCE JAR
PREP TIME: 15 MINUTES
STEEPING TIME: 3 MONTHS

2¼ pounds ripe, slightly firm cherries

3⅓ cups brandy

1½ cups super-fine sugar

1 cinnamon stick

1 sterilized jar (page 253)

1. Wash the cherries in cool water, let them drain, and dry them with a dish towel. Remove their stems.

2. Put the cherries in the jar and add the stick of cinnamon. Sprinkle the sugar over the cherries, and then pour in the brandy. Seal the jar tightly and store it in a cool, dark spot.

3. Let the cherries steep for about three months.

Preserves in brandy

The longer a fruit steeps in brandy, the tastier it becomes. Be patient and wait two to three months before opening your preserves. The results are worth the wait!

Fruit Paste Rounds
(Pâte de fruits rouge)

RECIPE SERVES 10 PEOPLE
PREP TIME: 30 MINUTES
COOKING TIME: 10 MINUTES
DRYING TIME: 12 HOURS

18 ounces fruit (blackberries, blackcurrants, blueberries, or redcurrants)
14 ounces jelly sugar (sugar with pectin)
½ cup granulated sugar

1. Wash and dry the fruit. Put it in a pan with 1 cup of water and heat it up until bubbles appear. Let the fruit bubble a bit. Then thoroughly crush the fruit into a pulp and put it through a strainer.

2. Transfer the strained pulp to a large, thick-bottomed pan, add the gelling sugar, and heat to a boil. Cook at a rolling boil for 10 minutes while stirring. When the liquid has evaporated and the paste thickens, remove the pan from the heat.

3. Line a baking sheet with wax paper. Spread the paste out on the paper with a flat spatula so that it's smooth. Let the paste dry for at least 12 hours.

4. Cut the paste into circles or squares with a sharp knife. Roll them in the granulated sugar and enjoy. You can store them in a lidded container or tin.

Quince Paste
(Pâte de coing)

RECIPE SERVES 6 PEOPLE
PREP TIME: 15 MINUTES
COOKING TIME: 35 MINUTES
SET ASIDE: 3 DAYS

1⅓ **pound quinces**

18 **ounces granulated sugar**

A bit of super-fine sugar

½ **cup water**

Food processor

1. Rinse the quinces in cool water and dry them. Cut them into quarters and put them in a jelly pan or large thick-bottomed pan. Add the water and bring it to a boil. Simmer the quince pieces for about 15 minutes. They should be tender to the touch after cooking.

2. Peel the quince pieces, remove their cores and seeds, and run them through a food processor (fine mesh).

3. Weigh the resulting pulp and put it in a jelly pan with the same weight of sugar. Bring the ingredients to a boil and then simmer them for 20 minutes, stirring them frequently. The fruit pulp will look compacted once it's cooked.

4. Cover a baking sheet with wax paper. Then spread the paste out on the sheet in a layer that's about ¾-inch thick. Let the paste set in a cool, dry spot for three days. Use a cookie cutter to cut shapes out of the paste and roll them in the super-fine sugar. Store in a container lined with wax paper.

Candied Ginger
(Gingembre confit)

RECIPE FILLS ONE 12-OUNCE JAR
PREP TIME: 20 MINUTES
COOKING TIME: 1½ HOURS

12 ounces fresh, peeled ginger
2½ cups of super-fine sugar
5 tablespoons water

1. Using a mandoline cutter or knife, cut the ginger into ¾-inch slices.

2. Put the slices into a thick-bottomed pan with 2 cups of the super-fine sugar and stir. Add the water and cook over low heat until the sugar dissolves. Let the mixture simmer for 90 minutes over very low heat, stirring occasionally.

3. Spread the rest of the sugar out on a piece of wax paper. Using a skimmer, remove the ginger slices from the pan and put them on the wax paper. Let the slices cool. (Tip: Save the syrup that remains in the pan and use it with other recipes.)

4. Roll the ginger slices around in the sugar until they're coated.

Candied Orange and Lemon
(Fruits confits orange et citron)

RECIPE MAKES 7 OUNCES
PREP TIME: 15 MINUTES
COOKING TIME: 1½ HOURS
SET ASIDE: 2 NIGHTS
DRYING TIME: 24 HOURS

4 oranges

4 lemons

1½ pounds super-fine sugar

4 cups water

1 tablespoon corn syrup

1. Wash all of the fruit. Cut two of the lemons and two of the oranges into quarters. Use a zester to peel some of the remaining fruit, creating thin strips of peel. Peel the rest of the fruit with a fruit-and-vegetable peeler, creating broader strips.

2. Bring a pot of water to a boil and add the quartered fruits and peels. Boil them uncovered for 10 minutes to remove any bitterness. Then take the fruit out of the water and let it drain on a paper towel.

3. Combine the sugar and water in another pot and bring them to a boil. Stir until the sugar is completely dissolved. Add the fruit and boil for 15 minutes over low heat, uncovered. Then take the fruit out of the pan with a fork and put it on a paper towel.

4. Let the syrup cool and then bring it to a boil again to thicken it. Put the fruit back in the syrup and cook it for 20 minutes. Take the pan off the heat and let the fruit steep in the syrup, covered, overnight.

5. On the following day, add the corn syrup to the mixture and put it back on the heat for 20 minutes. When bubbles start to appear, take the pan off the heat and let the fruit steep again overnight. The syrup should thicken substantially. To test it, dip your index finger in the syrup and rub it against your thumb. When you separate your fingers, the syrup should stretch out in a string of about an inch.

6. On the following day, repeat step 5 but do not add any more corn syrup. After 30 minutes of cooking, take the fruit out of the pan and let it cool on a rack. Place a napkin or baking sheet under the fruit to catch the syrup that drains out. Let the fruit dry for 8-12 hours, then store it covered in a cool, dark spot. Depending on their size, the oranges and lemons can take one to three weeks to candy properly.

Tips

• *Once the candied fruits are at their best consistency, they will stay that way for two to three weeks in a cool, dark spot. After that, they'll start to get harder and less enjoyable.*

• *Keep the syrup that's left over from the cooking process in a jar. It can be used in compotes and custards and as a base for ice cream.*

Soft Caramels
(Caramels mous)

RECIPE MAKES 36 CARAMELS
PREP TIME: 10 MINUTES
COOKING TIME: 20 MINUTES
REFRIGERATION TIME: 2 HOURS

1⅔ cups sugar

⅔ cup unsweetened evaporated milk

3½ tablespoons fresh, thick cream

¼ cup butter cut into cubes

½ teaspoon salt

1 teaspoon of vanilla extract

Candy thermometer

1. Line a square, 8-inch pan with wax paper.

2. In a large saucepan, mix the sugar, evaporated milk, cream, butter, and salt. Bring the mixture to a rolling boil and then turn down the heat and let it simmer for 15 minutes. The candy thermometer should reach a temperature of 240°F. Stir the mixture as it simmers. It must continue to cook at a rolling boil.

3. Remove the pan from the heat and vigorously beat the mixture with a whisk for three minutes. The caramel should lose its shininess and become grainy. Stir in the vanilla extract.

4. Pour the caramel into the pan lined with wax paper. Let it cool and then refrigerate it for at least two hours before cutting it into squares.

Vanilla Ice Cream
(Glace à la vanille)

RECIPE MAKES 1 QUART
PREP TIME: 5 MINUTES
COOKING TIME: 20 MINUTES
FREEZER TIME: 2 HOURS

3¼ cups milk

2½ cups super-fine sugar

1 vanilla pod

6 egg whites

7 tablespoons fresh cream

Ice-cream maker

1. Cut the vanilla pod lengthwise into two pieces and scrape out the seeds. Put the pod pieces, seeds, and milk in a saucepan and boil them for three minutes. Then let the mixture steep for 15 minutes.

2. Combine the egg yolks and sugar in a bowl. Whip until the mixture turns white and starts to foam. Add the milk from step 1 to the bowl and then pour the mixture back into the saucepan while stirring. Stir until the ingredients thicken into a custard. Then remove the pan from the heat, add the fresh cream, and mix thoroughly.

3. Pour the mixture into the ice-cream maker and follow its instructions.

4. Transfer the ice cream from the freezer to the refrigerator 30 minutes before serving so that it can soften a bit.

Chocolate Sorbet
(Sorbet au chocolat)

RECIPE MAKES 1 QUART
PREP TIME: 20 MINUTES + 20 MINUTES IN ICE-CREAM MAKER
COOKING TIME: 10 MINUTES
FREEZER TIME: 1 HOUR

9 ounces dark chocolate (70% cocoa content), grated

2½ tablespoons powdered cocoa

1½ cup super-fine sugar

Ice-cream maker

1. Put three cups of water into a pan and add the powdered cocoa and sugar. Mix the ingredients as they simmer. Let the mixture come to a low boil.

2. Add the grated chocolate. Continue to stir until all of the chocolate has melted and then remove the mixture from the burner and let it cool.

3. Pour the mixture into the ice-cream maker and follow its instructions.

4. Transfer the ice cream from the freezer to the refrigerator 30 minutes before serving so that it can soften a bit.

Ice cream with no machine

You can make ice cream even if you don't have a machine. Just put the ingredients into a large mixing bowl in the freezer for two hours. Take it out every fifteen minutes and whip the ingredients vigorously to keep ice flakes from forming.

Strawberry Ice Cream
(Glace à la fraise)

PREP TIME: 10 MINUTES
COOKING TIME: 20 MINUTES
TIME IN FREEZER: 2 HOURS

18 ounces strawberries with stems removed

2 cups milk

5 egg yolks

1 cup super-fine sugar

Juice of ½ lemon

7 tablespoons fresh cream

Food processor or blender

Ice-cream maker

1. Blend the strawberries in the food processor or blender and sprinkle them with the lemon juice. Then strain the strawberries to remove the seeds.

2. Boil the milk in a saucepan. Combine the egg yolks and sugar in a bowl and whip the mixture until it turns white. Add the boiled milk and stir continuously until the mixture thickens and coats your spoon. Let it cool down.

3. Stir the strawberry purée into the cream. Mix the ingredients thoroughly.

4. Pour the mixture into the ice-cream maker and follow its instructions.

5. Transfer the ice cream from the freezer to the refrigerator 30 minutes before serving so that it can soften a bit.

CHAPTER **10**

Beverages

wines, herbal teas, syrups...

MAKING SYRUP

fig. 1 : boiling juice + sugar ~ fig. 2 : straining ~ fig. 3 : bottling

Soy, Nut, and Coconut Milk
(Laits & co)

Soy Milk

RECIPE MAKES 1 QUART
PREP TIME: 30 MINUTES
STEEPING TIME: 8 HOURS OR OVERNIGHT

5 ounces dried soybeans

7 cups filtered water

1 pinch salt

Agave nectar, maple syrup, or honey

2 dried dates (optional)

Food processor or blender

Fine sieve or coffee filter

1. Rinse the soybeans several times in cold water. Let them soak overnight in two cups of filtered water. Then drain and rinse the soybeans again. Discard any loose skin.

2. Blend the soybeans with 5¼ cups of water for one minute, making sure you don't blend them too finely. Press the mixture through a very fine sieve or clean coffee filter with a bowl underneath it to catch the milk that comes out. Discard the soy pulp.

3. Boil the soy milk in a pan for about 10 minutes. Add the salt and sweeten to taste with the agave nectar, maple syrup, or honey. If you add the dried dates, remove the pits and then blend the dates with the milk until smooth.

4. Let the soymilk cool and then store it in a tightly sealed container in the fridge.

Nut Milk

RECIPE MAKES 1 QUART
PREP TIME: 30 MINUTES
STEEPING TIME: 8 HOURS OR OVERNIGHT

12 ounces shelled, unsalted almonds with skins

5¼ cups filtered water

1 pinch salt

Agave nectar, maple syrup, or honey

2 dried dates (optional)

Food processor or blender

Fine sieve or coffee filter

1. Rinse the nuts several times in cold water. Soak them overnight in 5¼ cups of filtered water. Blend them for one to two minutes. Don't blend them too finely.

2. Press the mixture through a very fine sieve or clean coffee filter with a bowl underneath it to catch the juice that comes out. Keep the pulp for use in other recipes—in a crumble or raw muesli.

3. Add the salt and sweeten the milk to taste. If you add the dried dates, remove the pits and then blend the dates with the milk until smooth.

4. Store in the refrigerator in a tightly sealed container.

Coconut Milk

RECIPE MAKES 1 QUART
PREP TIME: 15 MINUTES
STEEPING TIME: 5 MINUTES

18 ounces grated, unsweetened coconut

8 cups filtered water

1 pinch salt

Agave nectar, maple syrup, or honey

2 dried dates (optional)

Food processor or blender

Fine sieve or coffee filter

1. Boil two quarts of water. Put the coconut in a large saucepan and pour the boiling water over it. Let the coconut steep for about five minutes.

2. Press the mixture through a very fine sieve or clean coffee filter with a bowl underneath it to catch the milk that comes out.

3. Add the salt and sweeten the milk to taste. If you add the dried dates, remove the pits and then blend the dates with the milk until smooth.

4. Store the milk in the refrigerator in a tightly sealed container.

Dried Herbs and Flowers

1. The best time to gather herbs and plants is in the early morning during a spell of dry weather. Collect them right after the dew has formed and before the sun beats down on them. The essential oils that herbs and plants contain evaporate a bit each day with heat.

2. Dry the herbs and the plants you collect by spreading them out on a tray. Don't overlap them.

3. To preserve your herbs and plants, put them in jars or envelopes and store them in a dark, dry spot like a cupboard.

Thyme
(Thym)

Use small pruning shears to cut stalks of thyme. Then spread the stalks out on a tray in a dry place for a few days, turning them over regularly. Store the stalks in a tightly sealed container.

Verbena Leaves, Chamomile Flowers, or Cherry Stems
(Feuilles de verveine, fleurs de camomille)

Spread the leaves, flowers, or stems out on a tray in a dry spot. Stir them around regularly. Wait two weeks and then use or store the leaves in a tightly sealed container.

Cherry Stem Infusion
(Décoction de queues de cerises)

Cherry stems are known for their diuretic properties. See page 238 for instructions on drying cherry stems for an infusion.

1. Put a handful of cherry stems into one quart of water and boil them for 10 minutes.

2. Filter and enjoy the infusion while it's warm.

Chamomile Tea
(Infusion de camomille)

Chamomile has a very unique taste. Many people find that chamomile tea helps with digestion and relaxation.

1. Boil a cup of water.

2. Put five chamomile flowers in a cup with six to eight ounces of water just off the boil. Cover and steep for 10 minutes.

3. Remove the chamomile flowers and drink the tea hot.

Lemon Syrup
(Sirop de citron)

PREP TIME: 10 MINUTES
COOKING TIME: 15 MINUTES

4 cups lemon juice

Peel from 1 lemon

2¼ pounds of super-fine sugar

2 cups water

1. Put the water and super-fine sugar into a thick-bottomed pan and bring the mixture to a boil. Stir the mixture and let it bubble for two or three minutes. Then remove the pan from the heat and let the mixture cool down.

2. Transfer the syrup from step 1 to a bowl and add the lemon peel and lemon juice. Then pour this mixture back into the pan and heat it for five to 10 minutes, stirring regularly.

3. Let the mixture cool and filter it with a coffee filter. Let the syrup cool before bottling it.

Mint Syrup
(Sirop de menthe)

PREP TIME: 15 MINUTES
STEEPING TIME: 1 NIGHT
COOKING TIME: 15 MINUTES

4 bunches fresh mint

1 quart filtered water

2¼ pounds super-fine sugar

1. Separate the mint leaves, rinse them in cool water, and put them in a mixing bowl. Add boiling water to the bowl and cover it with plastic wrap. Let the mint leaves steep in the bowl overnight.

2. On the following day, filter the mint juice and pour it into a thick-bottomed pan.

3. Add the super-fine sugar and bring the mixture to a boil while stirring. Simmer for about 10 minutes and then remove the pan from the heat.

4. Let the syrup cool before bottling it.

Currant Syrup
(Sirop de cassis)

PREP TIME: 15 MINUTES
COOKING TIME: 5 MINUTES

4 cups currant juice

9 cups super-fine sugar

1. Combine the currant juice and super-fine sugar in a thick-bottomed pan and bring them to a boil. Stir the mixture while it simmers for two or three minutes. Then remove the pan from the heat and let it cool.

2. Filter the resulting syrup. Let it cool before bottling it.

Storing syrup
Syrups are best used right after they're made. They can be kept for about a month in the fridge.

Mulled Wine
(Vin chaud)

PREP TIME: 20 MINUTES
STEEPING TIME: 24 HOURS
COOKING TIME: 30 MINUTES

1 orange

1 clove

1 quart red wine, such as a peppery Côtes du Rhône

1 cinnamon stick

6 tablespoons brown sugar

Ground cinnamon

1. Pour the wine into a large bowl or pan. Wash the orange, stick the clove in it, and let it steep in the wine for 24 hours.

2. On the following day, remove the orange and pour the wine into a saucepan. Add the brown sugar and cinnamon stick to the wine and simmer it uncovered for 15 minutes.

3. Take the wine off the heat and let it steep for 10 minutes. Remove the cinnamon stick. Reheat the wine before serving. Add a sprinkle of ground cinnamon if desired.

Variation

Instead of brown sugar, use three tablespoons of syrup from the Candied Oranges recipe on page 228.

Walnut Wine
(Vin de noix)

PREP TIME: 10 MINUTES
STEEPING TIME: 1 MONTH

6 fresh green walnuts (generally available in May or June)
1 quart of sweet white wine
8½ ounces brandy
1½ cup super-fine sugar
Sterilized jar (page 253)

1. Cut the walnuts into quarters. Put them into the jar with the wine, brandy, and super-fine sugar.

2. Cap the jar and let the wine steep for about a month. Stir it from time to time. When the wine is ready, filter and bottle it. Serve it very cold as an apéritif.

Appendices

Index of Recipes

Breads and Brioches

Yogurts

Fresh Cheeses

Pasta

Condiments

Preserves

Charcuterie, Terrines, and Spreads

Jams, Compotes, and Spreads

Cookies and Sweets

Beverages

Glossary of Techniques

Blanching

Certain fruits and vegetables should be washed and blanched before they're preserved. Blanching is just placing them into boiling water for a brief period (from 30 seconds to two minutes) and quickly removing them. Blanching helps to preserve the color of fruits and vegetables, gets rid of bitter flavors, and loosens up skins for easy peeling. Fruits and vegetables should generally be rinsed and allowed to dry after blanching.

Brine

Brine is a mixture of water and salt that's used to preserve meat, fish, fruits, and vegetables.

Candying

A culinary technique that's been practiced since ancient times, candying is the preservation of fruit in sugar. During the candying process, fruit is submerged and cooked in a sugary syrup. The syrup absorbs and replaces the moisture that's present in the fruit. Most fruits can be candied in this fashion, but sturdy fruits like lemons and oranges are the most common. The candying process can take one to three weeks.

Canning (Preserves)

Canning is a technique for preserving food, usually fruits and vegetables. During the canning process, food is put into glass jars, which are then boiled to eliminate bacteria and prevent spoilage. When canning, try not to pack the jars too tightly. If you pour in a liquid, don't fill the jar to the brim. Leave at least a ½ inch of space at the top so that the seal of the jar doesn't burst or warp during boiling. To sterilize the jars, put them in a pot filled with water (make sure the water covers the jars completely) and boil them for 10 minutes.

Cheese Drainer

Cheese drainers and molds come in a variety of shapes and sizes. If you are using a yogurt maker to hold your cheese at temperature, find small molds that fit inside the container(s) for your yogurt maker. If you're using a larger glass form, such as a Pyrex® dish, and your oven, you can use a much larger cheese drainer. A variety of cooking supply stores sell cheese drainers and molds, and you can find them online at: http://www.cheesemaking.com/cheesemoldsandpresses.html

Compote

A mixture of fruit and sugar that's cooked quickly, a compote is similar to a jam but less sugary, which means it won't keep as long.

Dehydration

This technique involves dehydrating fruits and vegetables in order to keep them from rotting. Fruits and vegetables can be dried naturally in the sun or dehydrated in a conventional oven with the door partly open. Another option is a dehydrator, a machine that dries fruits, vegetables, herbs, and meats and uses less energy than an oven.

Filtering

In this book, filtering is just the removal of solids contained in a liquid. Filtering requires a piece of cheesecloth or muslin, a sieve, or a very fine strainer.

Hydration Rate

The success of your bread depends largely on achieving the right water-to-flour ratio. Known as the hydration rate, this ratio will vary depending on the bread machine you're using, the type of flour you're baking with (whole-grain flour requires more water), and the temperature of the room (the hotter the temperature, the more water that's needed).

Jam

Jam is a cooked mixture of fruit and sugar. When making jam, you should sterilize the jars you plan to store the jam in to prevent spoilage. As an added precaution, cap your jars of jam tightly and turn them upside down. This will prevent the formation of a layer of mold on the surface of the jam and allow the lids to seal more effectively.

Poolish

Poolish is a type of fermentation starter that allows bread to develop over the course of a few hours before mixing and baking. Breads made with a poolish often have a better aroma, texture, and flavor than "quick" breads. They also tend to keep longer.

Preserves in Natural Juices

No supplemental products are added to this type of preserve, so the jars containing these preserves should be sealed tightly and sterilized.

Preserves in Oil

Oil is a natural preservative that insulates food from the air and keeps it from oxidizing too quickly or developing mold. Preserves in oil are best used a month or two after they're made.

Preserves in Salt

Salt functions as an antiseptic: it prevents the development of microbes. Choose a sea salt when it comes time to cure a ham or preserve a batch of anchovies. Salt preserves are best used a month or two after they're made, though they will keep longer.

Preserves in Syrup

A syrup made of water and sugar (and perhaps flavored with cinnamon, vanilla, or an alcohol) is an effective preservative for fruit and will help it retain both flavor and color. Fruit preserved in syrup can be kept for a year. The syrup itself will keep for a month.

Preserves in Vinegar

Using vinegar as a preservative prevents the development of food-spoiling microbes. You should use a strong vinegar (one that's at least 7% acetic acid). Vinegar preserves are best used a month or two after they're made but can be kept longer.

Sterilizing Jars

Before making preserves, jams, or sauces, you should sterilize the jars you'll be storing them in. Wash and dry the jars first. Make sure there is no dirt or debris clinging to the surface. Then submerge them in a pot of salted water and boil them for 10 minutes. Remove them and let them dry on a clean dish towel. You can also sterilize jars by putting them in an oven heated to 230°F for five minutes.

Sterilizing Food in Jars

The second stage of sterilization comes after the food is tightly sealed in jars. Unless the food inside needs to be cooked longer, you typically submerge the jars in a pot of water and boil them for 10 minutes. The heat will force air out of the jars and prevent the development of mold. (You can also sterilize the jars using a pressure cooker or sterilizer.)

Yogurt Maker

This machine is just for making yogurt. It heats the necessary ingredients to the appropriate temperature and then maintains the temperature until yogurt forms and sets. Some yogurt makers have a switch and a timer that allow you to choose the length of each cycle. The time needed to make yogurt—between six and 16 hours—depends on climate, the yogurt starter, and the milk used.

Additional contributors to this book

Keda Black:
Tomato sauce page 70, pesto page 72. Flavored butters page 78. Flavored salts page 85. Homemade ketchup page 86. Mayonnaise page 88. Chips page 172.

Rachel Khoo:
Pâté de foie page 150. Tarama page 164. Hummus page 166. Chocolate-hazelnut spread page 192. White chocolate spread page 192. Chestnut cream page 194. Salted butter caramel page 196. Lemon curd page 198. Traditional muesli page 210. Winter muesli page 210. All-chocolate muesli page 210. No-cook cereal bars page 212. Traditional cereal bars page 212. Gluten-free granola page 213. Traditional granola page 214. Soy milk page 236. Nut milk page 236. Coconut milk page 236.

Marie Leteuré:
Chicken bouillon page 98. Beef bouillon page 100. Lamb bouillon page 102. Fish bouillon page 104. Vegetable bouillon page 106.

Delphine de Montalier:
Homemade smoked salmon page 162.

Laura Zavan:
Fresh egg pasta pages 62-64. Flavored pastas page 66. Cooking pasta page 68.

An Imprint of Sterling Publishing
387 Park Avenue South
New York, NY 10016

ISBN 978-1-4547-0858-2

Library of Congress Cataloging-in-Publication Data

Laurendon, Laurence.

 [Fait maison. English]

 From scratch : an introduction to French breads, cheeses, preserves, pickles, charcuterie, condiments, yogurts, sweets, and more / Laurence Laurendon, Gilles Laurendon, Catherine Quevremont, Cathy Ytak.

   pages cm

Includes bibliographical references and index.

Translation of Fait maison. Paris : Marabout (Hachette Livre), 2011.

ISBN 978-1-4547-0858-2 (alk. paper)

1. Cooking, French. I. Laurendon, Gilles. II. Quevremont, Catherine. III. Ytak, Cathy, 1962- IV. Title.

TX719.L374413 2014

641.5944--dc23

2013030977

Distributed in Canada by Sterling Publishing

c/o Canadian Manda Group, 165 Dufferin Street

Toronto, Ontario, Canada M6K 3H6

For information about custom editions, special sales, and premium and corporate purchases, please contact Sterling Special Sales at 800-805-5489 or specialsales@sterlingpublishing.com.

Manufactured in China

2 4 6 8 10 9 7 5 3 1

www.larkcrafts.com